THE VICTORY OF
THE CROSS

Desmond O'Grady is an Australian author and
journalist resident in Rome. He graduated from
the University of Melbourne and has taught
courses at the universities of Florence and Chieti.
His eight books include three volumes of fiction
and a biography. He has written for leading
newspapers and weeklies in England, the United
States, Australia and Italy.

The word "love" has been associated with the name of God only since Christ.

Paul Valery

DESMOND O'GRADY

THE VICTORY OF
THE CROSS

A HISTORY OF
THE EARLY CHURCH
IN ROME

HarperCollins*Religious*
An Imprint of HarperCollins*Publishers*

HarperCollins*Religious*
Part of HarperCollins*Publishers*
77–85 Fulham Palace Road,
Hammersmith, London W6 8JB

First published in Great Britain
in 1992 by HarperCollins*Religious*

1 3 5 7 9 10 8 6 4 2

Originally published in 1991 in the United States of America
by Our Sunday Visitor Publishing Division,
Our Sunday Visitor Inc.,
under the title *Caesar, Christ and Constantine*

A catalogue record for this book is
available from the British Library

ISBN 0 00 599322-9

Printed by Bell and Bain Ltd., Glasgow

For Kieran and Donatella

CONTENTS

The illustrations are used by courtesy of the Pontificia Commissione di Archaeologia Sacra; Fabbrica di San Pietro; Soprintendenza Archaeologica di Roma; and Desmond O'Grady.

INTRODUCTION

THIS book arose out of an article I wrote about the cemetery under St Peter's where the apostle's tomb is found. It showed that in Rome one can still see much that is related to the lives of the first Christians. For me, the cemetery was as interesting as Peter's tomb because it provided an insight into the Roman world in which Christianity took root.

That world bulks large in this book. One reason is that far more is available about it than about the early Christians, who acquire substance if shown in this context. Another reason is that part of my concern is with Rome's influence on the Christian movement.

After the first chapter which identifies the traces of early Christianity in modern Rome, there is a chronological account beginning with Augustus in which I continue to note what is extant from the first three centuries. The emperors' story, often bizarre, provides a thread, and with Constantine there is a point of convergence with the story of the Christians.

Histories of the early Church are legion, but this one concentrates on the Chrisian community in Rome. The main personages have some connection with the Roman Church. Of course, as the Constantinian era approached, the affairs of the Church in Rome became increasingly those of the Church at large.

Writing this book, I realized that not only are sites of the first three centuries intact but many situations of that period recur: an emperor-god died not long ago in Japan; New Age religious fads resemble some pagan cults; churches in Eastern Europe emerged recently after decades during which they were illegal and persecuted.

Eastern European churches survived against the state religion of atheism, whereas early Christians were often accused of atheism for not recognizing the many pagan gods. This might seem a decisive difference. But aren't today's Christians called to be atheists in respect to gods created by the media, corporate raiders exalted as symbols of success and others who, in various ways, demand veneration? In other words, Christians today still have to see through idols.

There are parallels between the first three centuries and today, but also differences not due solely to the early Christians' greater closeness to the source. Empathy has attempted to bridge the gap without inventing anything – at least not intentionally.

My thanks for help go to Mark Coleridge, who pointed out the hurdles, then helped me over them; to Gerald O'Collins, S.J., Henry A. Kelly and Edmund Campion.

1

DORMITORY OF
THE DEAD

TO climb the Capitoline Hill is to enter Rome's past
which was transformed into a Christian future. Here are
the remains of the temple of Jupiter Capitolinus (sixth
century BC), which was the centre of Rome's religious life;
moreover, in it the Senate annually held its first session. Here
ended all processions celebrating Rome's military triumphs.
Here was the hub of the city which became an empire.

Today the hill is crowned by the town hall complex
around Michaelangelo's piazza and the Church of Aracoeli,
built above the ruins of a temple dedicated to a pagan
mother-goddess. A medieval tradition claimed that where
the church now stands a Sibyl foretold Christ's coming to
the Emperor Augustus: *"Ecce ara primogeniti Dei"* – from
which the church takes its name, which means "Altar of
Heaven".

The piazza flanking the church was designed by Michelangelo in 1536 for the visit of an emperor who claimed a
link with Augustus but added a Christian sanction: the
Holy Roman Emperor Charles V, who was granted, for
defeating infidels in North Africa, a triumph modelled on
those of ancient Rome.

Charles's title harked back to the first Christian emperor,
Constantine. The equestrian statue in the centre of the
piazza was believed to be that of Constantine, which
accounts for its preservation through the Middle Ages. In

fact, it is of Marcus Aurelius, the emperor-philosopher whose tolerance did not extend to Christians. The melding of pagan and Christian is not untypical of Rome.

However, there are links with Constantine on the hill of the Capitol. In the Church of Aracoeli is an altar with a relic of his mother, St Helena, while in the courtyard of the Conservatori Palace, flanking the piazza, stand fragments of a forty-foot-high statue of the emperor – a huge head and also a hand with two fingers raised, perhaps in admonition or blessing. Previous emperors had believed the pagan gods ensured Rome's triumphs, but Constantine won in the Sign of the Cross. With him, Christ conquered the Capital, becoming *Christus Capitolinus*.

The Senatorial Palace, which closes the third side of the square, is the Town Hall. It is an example of bureaucratic continuity: through a glass wall within the building, one can see the remains of the *Tabularum* or Records Office dating from 78 BC. It is like looking into the entrails of history. A porphyry statue of Goddess Rome, spear in hand, helmet on head, stands before the building, whose façade bears an escutcheon with the proud cipher S.P.Q.R. – *Senatus Populesque Romanus* (the Roman Senate and People) – which is seen today also on municipal property such as buses and manhole covers. One of the several ribald current renderings of it is *Solo Preti Qui Regnano* (Only priests reign here).

Above this building is not the eagle of imperial Rome but the cross on which a Galilean preacher died a criminal's death during Augustus's reign. A flanking street descends towards the prison where, tradition has it, St Peter languished.

The Temple of Jupiter and other Capitoline buildings of ancient Roman times looked towards the Forum and the Colosseum. But now the Town hall, like the Church of

Aracoeli, looks out across rooftops and beyond the Tiber towards a dome which catches the light of the setting sun. The dome rises in a zone which in Augustus's time was uninhabited, a marshy tract beyond the city walls. But Constantine built a basilica there to mark the site where Peter, who had been given a mandate by the preacher who died a criminal's death, was buried after his execution during Nero's reign.

In St Peter's Basilica, on the feast of St Agnes (21st January) each year, two white lambs are presented to the pope. Decked with ribbons and flowers, they have been blessed previously on the tomb of Agnes, a fourth-century virgin-martyr, in the basilica dedicated to her on Via Nomentana. After presentation, the lambs are taken for shearing to the Benedictine nuns in nearby Trastevere. The nuns make their wool into pallia – narrow, stole-like strips with six black silk crosses, resembling an ancient Roman garment worn by philsophers and exponents of Greek culture. In church use, a pallium signifies authority.

Five months later, on 29th June, the feast of Sts Peter and Paul, when nets are draped from St Peter's façade in memory of the fishermen-apostles, the pope blesses the pallia. (It is worth noting that 29th June, a conventional date for Peter and Paul, is also that of the old pagan festival for Rome's legendary founders, Romulus and Remus.)

The blessed pallia are kept in a gilded silver casket, placed above Peter's tomb, until consigned to metropolitan archbishops. They symbolize the direct transmission of Peter's authority throughout the world, which is also underlined in official papal documents bearing the words *Datum Romae apud Sanctum Petrum*: "Given in Rome at St Peter's". The pallia are an example of Rome's "hands-on" aspect that makes it possible to touch the life of the first Christians; over almost two thousand years the continuity is unbroken.

St Peter's is situated where it is because Peter lies here: the main altar is built above his tomb site. Peter is the rock. This becomes evident beneath the basilica in the pagan necropolis where Peter was buried, probably in the year 64, after being killed in Nero's adjacent racecourse. Romans conceded burial rights to all except those found guilty of impiety toward the gods, as was the case with Christian martyrs. Their bodies were left at the mercy of the elements but could be claimed by friends. Presumably Peter found burial in this way. In the AD 90s his tomb was honoured, according to Julian, the emperor who, in the fourth century, reverted to paganism. "From the last decade of the first century," he wrote, "Peter's grave was already being venerated, in secrecy, it is true." About 120 a reinforcement wall was built around Peter's tomb. In 160 a red wall was built to enclose the area, and where it crossed Peter's grave a small shrine was erected, consisting of a travertine slab supported by two marble columns. At the back of the slab was a concave niche. It is claimed that when this was built Peter's bones were in the original tomb. This has all but vanished, presumably ransacked in the eighth century by Saracens seeking gold: two thousand Roman coins were found during the 1940s excavations, but the only gold was in a crack where looters would have overlooked it. Excavators found marks of the six flagstones which must have covered Peter's tomb. Part of a lamp and a tile from the reign of Vespasian (69–79) were excavated nearby, as was a drainage system whose tiles bore the stamp of Marcus Aurelius, titled as Caesar. Since he took the title of "Augustus" in 161, the tiles date from no later than 160. In subsequent transformations of the burial ground, trouble was taken to respect the tomb site.

At the beginning of the third century a Roman priest named Gaius referred to the site when he responded to a heretic with the claim "I can show you the shrines of the apostles who founded this church in the Vatican [the name of the site] and on the road to Ostia" (the site of St Paul's tomb). At the beginning of the fourth century, after his conversion, Emperor Constantine enclosed the shrine in a substantial marble structure before building the first St Peter's Basilica around and above it. Its top emerged from the basilica floor, and it, rather than an altar, became St Peter's focal point.

Excavations for a decade after 1939 were a calculated risk, as the thick pilasters which sustain the dome rest on this zone. It was the reverse of Emperor Constantine's operation and showed what he had let himself in for when he decided to build a huge church on a soggy hillside rather than on flat land nearby. Tradition has it that he himself carried twelve buckets of earth and turned twelve clods as workmen began to slice into Vatican hill. The workmen cut through the taller mausoleums and built a honeycomb structure between them, sustaining the basilica's floor. But first the empty spaces were filled with approximately two cubic tennis courts of earth, which was then tamped down. The work was done well, as the huge church lasted twelve hundred years before it was found that one side was sliding southward. Then, over a period of one hundred and twenty years, during which twenty-seven popes reigned, the present basilica was built. That Constantine was prepared to face these construction problems, and also the hostility of the pagan and Christian families whose tombs he despoiled, shows his conviction that the apostle was buried here.

Although Pius XII announced the discovery of Peter's tomb, and Paul VI the discovery of his bones, the excavations still remain controversial. Matters have not been helped by prima donna-like experts disagreeing about their findings and trying to upstage one another.

Imagination and information are needed to discern the shrine from AD 160 within the Constantinian casing, while Peter's bones are even more controversial than the tomb itself. There is some evidence for the tradition that to avoid robbery during the persecution of Valerian in 258, Peter's bones and those of Paul were transferred to St Sebastian's catacomb on the Appian Way. The hypothesis is that they were brought back in the 280s or immediately after Constantine's conversion, but rather than being put back in the original grave, they were placed this time in a niche in the "graffiti" wall, constructed about 260 over a crack in the Red Wall.

One hundred and thirty-five bones, some of them full-length, removed from the niche during the 1939–49 excavations and ignored for a decade, on examination proved to be those of a shortish, strongly-built man about seventy years old who had lived an outdoor life. The bones were wrapped in a gold-threaded purple cloth. There were no bones below the ankles, which would be the case if the man had been crucified upside down, as Peter was supposed to have been, and the corpse was cut away at the ankles. All this appeals to the imagination, although some archaeologists maintain that nothing can be proved from bones.

The wall outside the niche where the bones were found is covered with almost three hundred graffiti from the end of the third and beginning of the fourth century. One incomplete graffito, in Greek, on a piece of red plaster from inside the wall – "Petr eni" – probably meant "Peter is inside". None of those on the outside mention Peter, although what some claim is Peter's monogram (a "P" with a stylized key) is frequent.

The first- to fourth-century necropolis, measuring two hundred and thirty by sixty feet, more than thirty feet below the present basilica's floor, is a window into the pagan world which Christianity entered. What is visible was all built after Peter's burial. Probably there are also graves dating from before Peter's time at a level not excavated. Others were washed away by flooding which occurred most recently during the 1939–49 excavations. (The necropolis was much more extensive, but Constantine preserved only Peter's part.)

Christians, Egyptians and some Jews tended to bury corpses, but pagan Romans were more inclined to cremate them. However, as traditional religion's drab picture of the fortunes of the dead was eclipsed from the second century on by a stronger sense of individual survival, corpse burial became more common.

The necropolis's narrow streets are lined with individual or family tombs which have house-like façades. Some are freestanding, but most have continuous frontage. One hundred and five people, sixty-seven of them males, have been identified; some are buried in cinerary urns. Many are freed slaves who must have made money. There is a weaver, and a dealer in Spanish oil and wine, but most, such as an archivist who worked in Belgium, belonged to the public administration. The only noble is the daughter of Senator Ostorius Euhordianum whose name, Cheledon, means "a swallow". Traces of her purple dress were found in her tomb, and also a heavy gold bracelet.

The house-tombs consist of oblong chambers of concrete faced with brick. The decoration of their vaulted roofs and niches is deteriorating rapidly, mainly because of the more than thirty thousand people who visit the excavations yearly. Some of the twenty-two mausoleums are on two levels, having a terrace above with internal stairs. Most have marble sarcophagi. Families could close the chambers' heavy travertine doors, pray for their deceased, eat a meal as if he or she were present, then pour wine and perfumes into the coffin through apposite pipes or holes. The wine was for the deceased, the perfume to reduce the charnel smell.

An Egyptian family's mausoleum dates from the late-first century when Rome-Egyptian commercial and religious links were strong: an Egyptian priest accompanied Emperor Marcus Aurelius in his mid-European campaigns. An Egyptian divinity, Horus, in native costume, decorates one tomb of the mausoleum; Dionysius, who Romans believed accompanied their dead, decorates another; and a third tomb of a woman has an inscription indicating she was Christian. Horus, Dionysius and Christ all in one mausoleum make it a brief conspectus of mid-second-century Mediterranean religion.

Fannia Redempta (Redeemed), wife of a freedman of Emperor Diocletian, her name perhaps indicating she was a Christian, occupies a tomb with an outer courtyard. Her epitaph states she was married at thirteen and died at the age of forty-six years, five months and seven days. (Another tomb indicates its male Christian occupant lived thirty-one years, four months, ten days, and three hours.)

Most tombs are pagan, but a mid-second-century tomb near Peter's, whose title plate attests that half of it was sold during construction for a special interment, is that of a martyr, to judge from the decoration of laurel wreath, chalice and lamp. Nothing is known about its occupant, nineteen-year-old Claudius Romanus, except that his parents purchased this site for him.

One Christian, Aemilia Gorgonia, is buried in the mausoleum of the Caetennii family. (It is claimed that the contemporary, aristocratic Caetarni family, which has produced two cardinals, is the same as that of this mausoleum, but some historians deny it.) Her husband's epitaph praises sweet Gorgonia's beauty and chastity, expressing the hope that she will sleep in peace. She is depicted drawing water from the well of (everlasting) life; the decoration is completed by doves bearing olive branches and the inscription "dormit in pace".

In the next-door-but-one mausoleum of the Valerian family, pre-Constantinian writing found on the wall reads: "Peter, pray to Christ Jesus for those pious people buried near your body." The greater incidence of Christian tombs close to that claimed to be Peter's is a further pointer to its authenticity.

The mid-third-century Julii chamber, which contains among others the tomb of a two-year-old girl, was initially pagan, but evidently its owners became Christian. The wall decorations include Jonah and the whale, very popular with early Christians, the Fisher of Men, and the Good Shepherd. In the vault mosaic, amid stylized green and black leaves, Christ rises in a chariot toward the sun. He resembles an emperor enjoying his apotheosis or, even more, the Sun god, for sun rays cross behind his head. Some scholars see this as evidence of a protracted confusion between the Sun god and Christ. It is claimed that belief in a Sun god was a form of monotheism which became a bridge to Christianity. However, another plausible explanation is that the tomb owner did not want to broadcast his allegiance to Christ too blatantly. The mosaic dates from about the mid-third century (which makes it the first known Christian mosaic), at a time when persecution was in the air. Christians had good reason to camouflage their allegiance. This would explain why it is necesary to look closely to see that the sun rays behind the Christ-figure's head form a cross.

Peter's grave, like those of other first-century Christians, was in a pagan necropolis outside the city walls. It was an open-air burial site, washed by rain and baked by sun, until Constantine covered it. Like other necropolises, the Vatican graveyard faced a major road, the via Cornelia, for pagan Romans believed they would continue to live as long as passers-by remembered them. The "queen of roads" was the Appian Way, where some of the mausoleums are still visible, such as the one Maxentius built for his son Romulus shortly before Constantine defeated him. The tombs in a roadside necropolis often were built alongside an underground chamber or two, reached by steps and protected by a fence, which made them more secure than ground-level tombs. There were none in the Vatican necropolis because the natural water level was too high.

When wealthy owners allowed their Christian slaves to be buried on their land, or became Christians themselves and opened their land for the burial of fellow believers, at first they used surface tombs, some of which had underground chambers. Needing more space – as they did not recycle their tombs – they extended the underground chambers into long galleries and sometimes linked them. These are the catacombs. As the galleries could not go beyond the boundaries of the land above, they were excavated at ever deeper levels. Many-tiered galleries spread out for kilometres. There are as many as eight levels from floor to roof in which niches were cut according to the size of the corpse. The body, in a winding sheet, was laid in the niche and closed off hermetically with tiles or a marble slab. There were air vents and skylights, but also fixtures by the tombs to hold lamps or torches. Larger recesses were used for family tombs, while there were rooms which could take up to sixty people for a eucharistic celebration. The catacombs were not refuges during persecution; Roman authorities knew their location.

The usual explanation of the word "catacomb" is that it derives from a quarry site on the Appian Way where the St Sebastian Basilica now stands, called "Catacumbas". There were catacombs in other places, such a Bolsena outside Rome, Naples, Syracuse and Tunisia, but Rome has no fewer than seventy Christian and six Jewish catacombs, which some scholars claim were the models for the Christian ones. Four are listed in the telephone directory, and one runs under the Saudi Arabian embassy. The prevalent volcanic stone, compact tufa, facilitated their excavation, because, when hacked, it comes away in chunks like Parmesan cheese.

In some places, such as St Sebastian's, catacombs and necropolises are found together. It is interesting, as in other aspects of the early Church, to discover if, where and when new elements were introduced by Christianity.

Pagans used the term "necropolis", or city of the dead, but Christians preferred "cemetery", which simply means "dormitory". For them the dead were simply sleeping in the Lord until the resurrection. Another difference was that while pagans commemorated the dead on their birthday or a kind of All Souls Day, Christians celebrated the deceased's death day, since for them this was birth to eternal life. The pagan and Christian *refrigeria* or commemorative meals may not have differed greatly. They seem to have been a combination of wake and picnic. Those commemorating their dead had probably walked quite a way, as burials had to be outside city walls, and found they needed a snack. Perhaps, as structures at St Sebastian catacombs suggest, the repast was taken on terraces on top of the mausoleums. The amount of wine which flowed may have been a constant, whether the ceremony was pagan or Christian. Some catacomb frescoes suggest it was copious.

Inscriptions on pagan tombs could be proud, prim or insouciant-illogical on the lines of "I was here, I am no more, I don't care". Often they carried generic wishes for the deceased, wherever he might be. Christian inscriptions, however, have a serenity deriving from the certainty Christ gave. For Christians, the darkness of the catacombs was illuminated by an other-wordly light.

A husband paid a tribute to his "worthy" wife, Aurelia, who had died at the age of twenty-eight: "I loved her as a wife for nine years without her causing me any bitterness. Keep well, dear. Be in peace with the blessed souls. Stay serene in Christ!" A deacon named Severus affirmed that his nine-year-old daughter would live until she rose again and "the Lord gives her spiritual glory."

Along with pagan names such as Hercules, Eros and Achilles, there are names which relect the new faith: Hope (Spes), Reborn (Renatus), Resurrection (Anastasia) and Pentecost.

Catacomb wall paintings, stucco reliefs and mosaics are usually not great works of art, but nevertheless they witness poignantly. Bread and wine are depicted in a basket above a fish, symbol of the Christ they become; Lazarus responds uncertainly to the new life Christ has given; Moses is present, as well as Peter and Paul. The art is Roman, but the subjects are new. The first depiction of Mary is found in the catacomb of Priscilla on Via Salaria.

Perhaps because it is behind a high wall and is run by nuns, this catacomb gives the idea that it is still family land. A certain Priscilla, who is buried on the site, made the land available in the second half of the second century. She was of the prominent Acili family, one of whose members, Acilius Glabrio, was exiled by the Emperor Domitian (81–96) for what seems to have been his Christian faith. Several martyrs and two popes – Marcellinus (296–303) and Marcellus (308–309) – are buried here.

The first official church cemetery was the St Callistus catacomb, given to the Church, probably by the family of the patroness of music St Cecilia, early in the third century. It is at the beginning of the Appian Way, where there are forty catacombs within a few kilometres of the Aurelian Wall; the area is honeycombed with the dear departed, Christians awaiting the resurrection. With its umbrella pines and oleander bushes, St Callistus seems far from the cars speeding along the flanking roads. It has four catacombs, two of which are linked, covering twenty kilometres in all. Approximately half a million early Christians are buried here; by extrapolation, one should be able to reach a reasonably accurate figure for the number of Christians in Rome before Constantine's conversion, but this has not been attempted. Many third-century popes are buried in St Callistus: in all there are fifty-six martyrs and eighteen other saints.

Alongside the St Callistus complex are the Catacombs and Basilica of St Sebastian, where there was a particular veneration of Sts Peter and Paul – whose remains, or part of them as mentioned, were thought to have been brought here temporarily in the third century. About 340 a basilica was built to mark the spot, but the present church was erected later.

The first church to be built in Rome was St John's, the cathedral of the bishop of Rome (the Pope). It marked the beginning of an ambitious church-building programme by Constantine – a startling change, as previously there had been no recognizable church buildings. St John's was built on Constantine's private estate. The site had belonged to a wealthy family called Laterani which accounts for the cathedral's full name St John Lateran. Like most of the city's churches, it has been substantially rebuilt; it incorporates bronze doors from the building which housed the Roman Senate, a body tenaciously opposed to Christianity. Nearby, on the site of the palace of Constantine's mother, St Helena, is the Holy-Cross-in-Jerusalem Basilica, which conserves what are claimed to be fragments of the True Cross brought back by Helena from the Holy Land.

St Paul's-Outside-the-Walls is built above the tomb of the apostle who was decapitated nearby. (Incidentally, this third St Paul's, rebuilt in the nineteenth century with the same dimensions as the second, is similar to the first St Peter's.) Beautiful St Lawrence-Outside-the-Walls rises above the Roman church's treasurer, whose alleged comment as he was literally grilled in 258 is a prize example of keeping one's cool: "Turn me over, I'm roasted on this side".

Individual sites tell only part of the story. The urban layout as a whole is eloquent: Constantine's churches were by or beyond the city walls, while the centre remained persistently pagan. Now, of course, there is a plethora of churches in central Rome, but for many years after Constantine's conversion its civic (and pagan) core remained intact. To make a Christian capital, he transferred to Constantinople.

Christianity was vigorous in Rome before Constantine's arrival. Originally, Christians met in one another's houses for the Eucharist; but it seems that by the middle of the third century there were houses entirely devoted to church activities. Remains of ancient Roman houses under churches such as St Pudentiana and St Martin ai Monti are probably those of house churches; pre-Constantinian, Pompeian-style frescoes are visible below St Martin's. It seems that by the beginning of the second century there was a room set aside for Christian worship in the house under what is now St Clement's. Beneath Sts John and Paul on the Caelian hill are rooms used for Christian burials in the early fourth century, when it was legally permissible to bury within the city walls only members of the imperial family and Vestal virgins, an élite group of pagan nuns.

Almost certainly Roman Christianity began among convert Jews who squabbled in their synagogues about the news from Palestine. Rome has Europe's oldest Jewish community. When word seeped through about an alleged Messiah, they lived on both sides of the Tiber level with the upriver port. Today much of the Jewish community is in the same zone, but on only one side of the river, between the Tiber island and Capitoline hill.

The pagan world into which Christianity entered lives on in Rome. It is claimed that the classical bust attached to the wall of Palazzetto Venezia, known by Romans as "Madama Lucrezia", came from the temple to the Oriental gods Isis and Serapis, which stood near the Pantheon. A first-century AD basilica near Rome's central railway station was devoted to the neo-Pythagorean cult, which proposed the transmigration of souls.

Of the oriental cults which competed with Christianity, the most tangible today is that of the Persian sun god Mithras, who was popular in the Roman army. There were fifty Mithraic temples in Rome before Constantine's conversion. Remains of Mithraic temples can be found under St Clement's and St Prisca's, which suggests the two religions were competing until Christianity got the upper hand.

What of Rome's traditional religion? One can imbibe the spirit of the place, harken to names such as Janiculum (hill of Janus), or visit the Pantheon, the almost intact temple of the major gods. The Capitol-Forum-Palatine area is redolent with religion. Imagination can carry one beyond the isolated columns and broken masonry to the time when the Forum area was merely a swamp between two hills overlooking the Tiber.

The remains of the temple of Vesta, the goddess of the hearth, is witness to a cult which lasted a millennium. The temple's circular shape is thought to derive from the thatched homes of the period of Rome's founder, Romulus. The six Vestal virgins, the remains of whose convent with an internal garden can still be seen, guarded objects supposed to prove that Rome had been founded by the survivors of the destruction of Troy. The Vestals' convent is noteworthy not only because the cult began early, but because it finished late: it was abolished only at the end of the fourth century, eighty years after Constantine's conversion. The name and inscription on a Vestal's statue in the convent's atrium have been erased, but the calm, determined face is believed to be that of Claudia, a Vestal who converted to Christianity in 364 and became a traitor to her fellow-priestesses. The convent stands near what is thought to be the house of Numa Pompilus (716–683 77 BC), the priest-king who founded Rome's civil religion. He was the Pontifex Maximus, head of the twelve-man college of priests. Among other things, they were reponsible for the all-important bridges across the Tiber (*pontifex* means bridge-builder).

Also close to the convent are three Corinthian columns of the temple of Castor and Pollux, dedicated in 484 BC to the brothers of Helen of Troy, who brought news that the monarchist attempt to regain power had failed. The temple celebrated the end of the monarchical era, which had lasted 244 years, and the beginning of the Republic which was to last twice as long. (The subsequent imperial era also lasted about 500 years.)

The Basilica Julia and the Rostra, both begun by Julius Caesar and completed by his nephew and successor Octavian (known later as Augustus), mark another stage of Roman religion and history. Julius Caesar, who did not hesitate to name a month after himself, modified the Forum. It had been an open space, like the main piazza of a present-day Italian town, which was the centre of the community's religious, commercial and political life. Caesar enlarged and embellished it but also reduced the public space with monumental buildings. After his assassination by those who feared he was subverting republican ideals, his body was brought to the Forum to lie in state. Mark Antony's commemorative speech to friends, Romans and countrymen inspired the crowd to make an improvised pyre on which the Republic was burned, and from its ashes emerged an emperor-god.

A temple and a column, whose remains still stand, were erected on the spot, the first monument in the Forum to a mortal man. A cult of the deified emperor was contrary to the spirit of a zone in which Senate and people exercised civil liberty. In fact, the proud rule of Senate and people was to be replaced gradually by that of the Emperor Augustus from the Palatine hill overlooking the Forum. His residence on the Palatine can still be visited, and the small decorated study, where he retired before taking major decisions, has recently been reconstructed.

My central-city bus stop is beside the mausoleum which Augustus built in 27 BC for himself, his family and succeeding emperors. The mausoleum consists of three concentric circles of brickwork, but as grass grows between them and it is surrounded by cypresses, it is like a restful Etruscan mound tomb. Flanking it on the Tiber bank, within a Rotary-financed glass structure, is the Altar of Peace built to celebrate the emperor's victories in Spain and Gaul, but also to mark the end of civil strife which had lasted for decades. It was peace after centuries of struggle to establish an empire. A marble screen around the altar has a bas-relief showing Aeneas (once again the umbilical cord to a more venerable culture), vegetable motifs, and Augustus with family members and pagan priests at the consecration ceremonies on 4th July, 13 BC. The monument celebrated the success of Rome and of its civil religion, but soon after, in one of its outer provinces – Galilee – a movement would begin which would give religion a new meaning. It would transform Rome but also be shaped by it.

2

FEELING DIVINE

AUGUSTUS Caesar's mausoleum is now red brick, but as he lay dying he boasted that he "had found a city of brick and left a city of marble". He established a rectangular forum in which the remains of his temple of Mars is still visible. The forum was dominated by Augustus's statue set among those of other great men beginning with Aeneas and Romulus. He built the imposing theatre of Marcellus, whose upper floors now contain luxury apartments, and the portico of Octavia bordering the Jewish quarter. In Augustus's honour, his son-in-law Agrippa built the Pantheon.

In his reign of more that forty years, Augustus had time to construct a city worthy to be capital of an empire. At his death in AD 14, the city probably had eight hundred thousand inhabitants in an empire of thirty-five million, about five million of whom were Roman citizens.

The Roman historian Suetonius described Augustus as handsome and well-proportioned but shortish. He had fair, curly hair, and outdoors he wore a broad-brimmed hat. He enjoyed watching boxing matches, gladiatorial shows, and playing dice. Initially ruthless, he later mellowed – although not with his adulterous daughter Julia, whom he sentenced to a harsh exile. He was a traditionalist even in dress: he wore homespun clothes. But this thoroughgoing conservative was also, perhaps despite himself, a political and religious innovator.

In 44 BC Julius Caesar had been assassinated by those who

believed his accumulation of powers subverted republican ideals. Octavian, winner of the subsequent power struggle against Brutus, Cassius and, later, Mark Antony, was hailed as saviour of Rome and restorer of the Republic. He resigned all his powers, but in 27 BC, when he was thirty-six, the Senate bestowed on him the title "Augustus", which became his name. Corresponding roughly to "Venerable", it had religious connotations. It was still being used as a title by those who claimed to be heirs of the Roman emperors (the Habsburgs) eighteen hundred years later. The Senate also gave him control of the frontier provinces and the army there: in other words, he was emperor, which originally meant commander-in-chief. In fact, the commander of the army commanded everything. As if this were not more than enough, he had other powers, such as the right to veto senatorial laws. Republican forms were preserved. His rule was called the Principate, as he was the Princeps, the Senate's chief executive officer, whose powers were granted only in instalments and could be withdrawn. But, in fact, the Restorer of the republic had become an unconstitutional monarch. It would have been better if his monarchical role were recognized and some safeguards introduced.

The same was true in the religious sphere. Here also Augustus seemed a traditionalist intent on restoring the old-time religion. He built over eighty temples in and near Rome while restoring others, reviving traditional festivals and cults such as that of Castor and Pollux, as well as priestly colleges.

So far, so traditional. But as well as reviving religious feast days, he added holidays celebrating major events of his family, such as births and victories. When they coincided with religious feast days, the family celebrations took precedence, which indicates Augustus's priorities. Sacrifices had always been offered for Rome's success; now that

Rome was personified by the emperor, it was natural that homage be paid to him as embodiment of the State. It was homage to the emperor's guiding spirit, to the god made manifest through him rather than to him as a god incarnate.

Augustus did not want a cult addressed to him personally, but in each of Rome's fourteen districts there was a shrine where the emperor's genius or guiding spirit could be honoured. He did not want temples to him built in the provinces unless his cult was linked with that of Rome, an indication that he wanted devotion to the State rather than to him personally. But it was not always possible to separate these two aspects, and perhaps Augustus, for all his coyness about being the first god in a broad-brimmed hat, did not really want to.

Augustus a god? He was there or thereabouts: he was of the Julian family, which traced its origins to the goddess Venus, and nephew of a lesser god, Julius Caesar, whose temple in the Forum was served by an order of priests. If divinity was identified with power, Augustus was it. Moreover, while gods were distant, the ruler-god's might was manifest immediately. As Horace wrote:

Jove [Jupiter] we call King, whose bolts rive heaven:
Then a god's presence shall be felt
In Caesar [i.e., the ruler], with whose power the Celt
And Parthian stout in vain have striven.

The emperor cult meant different things in different times and places, just as in the twentieth century to be standing in a cinema during the playing of "God save the Queen" meant different things in Coventry and Calcutta. In the East, where there was a tradition of ruler-cults, people sought god-kings; Rome, however, had a republican tradition, but everywhere the emperor-cult could be used as a loyalty test.

Homage to the emperor was not the same thing as the Senate's granting an apotheosis (canonization) or decreeing damnation of emperors after their death. The Senate execrated the memory (*damnatio memoriae*) of bad emperors such as Nero, who ultimately were a threat to the State's prestige and stability. It was the Senate's chance for revenge after humiliation. Senators who, at a gladiatorial show, had been obliged to chant to Commodus, "You are the Lord, the Foremost and Most Blessed of Men", after his death changed their tune to "Enemy of the Senate, Enemy of the Gods. . . ."

Some emperors did not wait for the Senate's verdict but brazenly declared themselves gods rather than letting the concept adhere to them. Those whom the gods wished to destroy, it could be said, they first made gods. Caligula ran the whole gamut: one day he was Venus, another day Minerva and the next Jupiter, or the Good Goddess.

Poets had a role in the creation of the imperial cult, although it is not always easy to say whether they wrote in a paroxysm of servility, were employing literary conventions, were simply buttering-up emperors to nudge them in a certain direction, or were sincere in their tributes. Probably they were the tip of an iceberg of flunkeydom, which could induce any man to believe he was a god. Martial's satirical bite disappeared when he welcomed Domitian back to Rome:

Come then, O Caesar, e'en though it be by night;
Let the stars keep their stations for the sight:
Come and your people shall not want for light.

The poet Lucan claimed Nero could alter the balance of the universe; the emperor later had him killed, not for exaggeration in his lacklustre verse, but for winning a poetry contest the emperor had entered.

Some emperors had a tongue-in-cheek attitude toward the whole concept. Tiberius restrained Spaniards who wanted to erect a temple in his honour. He called on the Senate to witness that he was a mortal. When Claudius was killed by poisoned mushrooms, his adoptive son Nero remarked with ghoulish humour that mushrooms must be the food of the gods, as they had transformed a fool such as Claudius into one. As Vespasian lay dying, he said (and one can sense an accompanying wink), "I feel I'm becoming a god". His attitude seems to have been that if the likes of Nero were gods, it was hard to keep a straight face. Seneca was to refer to the divinization of the Emperor Claudius as his "Pumpkinification".

The drift toward a ruler-cult and unbridled political power was masked under Augustus by his homespun style, suggested by the fact that despite his powers he continued to live in a relatively modest house on the Palatine (though his modesty did not stop him from emulating his uncle by naming a month after himself). Writers and image-makers collaborated in the construction of a consensus about the Restorer of the Republic who buried it, reducing opportunities for the emergence of rivals and possibilities for expression of public opinion.

In both politics and religion, one factor pushing Augustus in a direction he might not have desired personally was the empire. Rome's gods were identified with the city itself, whereas the emperor-cult had an appeal from Mauretania to Syria. It was acknowledgement of the state power which held together myriad peoples of diverse religious traditions.

The empire had been created and was sustained by the army. Both empire and army had seemed merely expressions of Rome, but now they were shaping it. The army was the basic structure of a warrior state in which all senior positions were held by army officers: prominent citizens

B

passed from pleading court cases to leading armies to presiding over religious rites which, as magistrates, they conducted. Initially the army consisted of Italian peasants attached to Rome, but progressively they were replaced by those from outer provinces more responsive to an emperor than to Rome. The army, and its commander-in-chief the emperor, outweighed the Senate which pretended to rule.

In other words, Rome could no longer behave as if it were a city-state rather than an immense empire. It needed a ruler with broad powers and a cult which could unify diverse peoples.

Augustus's undeniable qualities hid the problems implicit in the developments he set in course. He was shrewd and sober, striking an admirable balance between Rome's peasant origins and urbanity. But what if his vast powers were wielded by a lesser man, a villain or madman?

The failure to acknowlege the drift he had set in motion and to provide checks was dangerous, particularly as the Julian-Claudian family had a flair for choosing worthless heirs. But the negative consequences emerged only gradually. Many Romans were convinced they had never had it so good as during Augustus's reign. It has been claimed that Virgil's Fourth Eclogue prefigures Christ by forecasting the birth of a child who would restore the Golden Age. It is more likely, however, that it refers to the birth of an heir to Augustus, because many Romans believed he had introduced an unending halcyon era.

3

FROM TARSUS
TO TRASTEVERE

VISITORS from Rome, as the Acts of the Apostles recounts, heard the apostles speak in tongues at the first Pentecost in Jerusalem. Presumably the visitors were Jews, and some of them brought Christianity to Rome, where the first Jewish community in Europe had been established in the second century BC. By the early first century there were about fifty thousand Jews in Rome, and they maintained regular contact with Jerusalem.

It would have been in Rome's twelve synagogues, which had no central authority, that Jews told their brethren about Jesus as the fulfilment of the prophecies. In many cities the claim that Jesus was the Messiah caused clashes, and Rome seems to have been no exception: Emperor Claudius, in AD 49, expelled Jews because of disturbances among them over a certain "Chrestus", which was probably a mis-spelling of Christ. A tentmaker named Aquila, originally from Pontus in what is now Turkey, and his wife Prisca, the first Christians of Rome whose names are known, were among this group. They were to figure later in Christianity's development.

Despite Claudius's reprisal for tumults over "Chrestus", Christiniaty won followers in Rome. It caught on in Jewish districts such as that near the Tiber port, but in the cosmopolitan city it spread also among Greek-speaking immigrants workers, some of whom had probably met

Christians in their homeland. If Christian on their arrival, they would have brought the brand of Christianity known in their community of origin and sought others of the same background. Some matrons in wealthier districts, such as the Aventine hill opposite the Palatine, were early Christians; they were able to respond more readily than men, who were restrained by their public life and offices. Doubtless conversion created difficulties for some in daily life, as they could not have anything to do with pagan games and ceremonies, or connected trades such as idol-making. Some families must have been split by conversion.

Christians did not need structures to live their faith: they swam easily in pagan waters. They needed no temples, since the Eucharist could be celebrated anywhere. Pagans required stone altars for sacrifice, but any old table sufficed for Christians. There was no clerical garb. At first sight, nothing distinguished Christians from their neighbours.

Much has to be stripped from present-day Catholicism, and a little added, to find the religion of Rome's first Christians. As well as not having churches, they did not celebrate Christmas or Easter with particular emphasis. They had no gospels, as they were yet to be written. Doctrine was in a nascent state. There was no pope as now known. The Vatican was a peripheral zone of Rome rather than a city-state.

Presumably the Lord's Prayer ("Our Father") was known, but other prayers, though focused on Christ and his redemption, were still similar to those of the Jews. Christians praying to the God of Abraham, Isaac and Jacob considered him the Father of Jesus Christ. The Apostles' Creed had not yet been formulated. It is hard to find references to Mary by the first Christians in Rome.

The liturgical language was Greek. Baptism, preceded by a catechumenate of several years, was the Christians' schooling. It was the passage from the pagan world to a new life which would continue after death.

There was the excitement of the recent revelation in Palestine, the stories of those who had known the Messiah or his disciples, a conviction that the Second Coming was imminent. The Christian movement had only a brief history, but what it had gave a direction to history itself. In addition, it had not been compromised with worldly powers. By AD 58, within three decades of Christ's death, the Christian community in Rome had achieved a certain renown, to judge by a letter which a deaconess called Phoebe brought to it from Corinth. Possibly she climbed the Aventine hill to deliver it to her Corinthian acquaintances Aquila and Prisca, who lived there, according to legend, opposite the imperial residences on the Palatine. The letter said of the Christians in Rome, "Your faith is proclaimed in all the world" – high praise indeed. The correspondent was Paul of Tarsus.

Paul had been Saul when he left the Jewish colony of Tarsus, a cosmopolitan trading town in what is now Turkey, for Jerusalem. Under Herod, Jerusalem had become a handsome city of some forty thousand inhabitants in which the Temple, reconstructed in 19 BC, had pride of place.

Saul had studied with Rabbi Gamaliel, renowned as a strict, upright Pharisee, from the time of the youth's arrival in Jerusalem in the year 14. Gamaliel must have honed Paul's considerable dialectical skills. In the year 26 Pontius Pilate was nominated prefect of Judea; John the Baptist was about to begin preaching.

As a student Saul did not seem to notice that Jesus and his disciples came to Jerusalem for Passover each year, nor even that the Galilean was condemned there in the year 30. But in Jerusalem's Supreme Council, the Sanhedrin, his mentor

Gamaliel, asked about reports of the risen Christ's followers, said that "if this plan or this undertaking is of men, it will fail; but if it is of God, you will not be able to overthrow them."

Saul was on the spot when Stephen, a Christian deacon whose task was to help the poor, was stoned to death after condemnation by the Jewish religious authorities. Saul approved; indeed the zealous young Pharisee became an implacable persecutor of Christians. In Jerusalem he sought them door-to-door and had many imprisoned. He wanted their total destruction, but Peter, John, Philip and others were already making converts outside Jerusalem. They were even baptizing Samaritans, the Jews' worst enemies. There were alarming reports of followers of the Nazarene causing trouble in the Damascus synagogue. Saul, who was about thirty, was sent to combat Christians there. But on the road, he recounted later, he was confronted by Jesus. He recognized that Jesus was not, as he had previously believed, someone who died on the cross cursed by God, but the Saviour of the world. Perhaps Saul recalled Gamaliel's words, "if this is God's work, nothing can stop it". Saul was baptized as Paul. And from that moment, nothing could stop him.

No one needed to teach him about Christianity: he had studied it as an enemy, now he saw it in the light of Christ. When the ex-Pharisee and persecutor of Christians proclaimed that Jesus was the Son of God, he "threw the Jews who lived in Damascus into complete confusion". To avoid an assassination plot, he had to flee the city.

It was a story repeated elsewhere: Paul turning synagogues into hornets' nests, making some converts, then resuming his travels. His opponents called his followers "men who have turned the world upside down".

Early in the year 50, in Corinth in the Peloponnesos, Paul

met Aquila and Prisca, a couple expelled from Rome the previous year. Sharing the same trade, tent-making, and the same faith, they became firm friends. Paul lived wih Aquila and Prisca, and later he wrote that they were "my fellow workers in Christ Jesus, who risked their necks for my life" (Romans 16:4).

In Corinth, not for the first or last time, Paul felt himself at the end of his tether with the Jews who were deaf to Jesus, while the Jews, for their part, were fed up with the turncoat Paul. They hauled him before the governor Junius Annaeus Gallio, the elder brother of the Stoic philosopher Seneca. They complained that Paul was encouraging people to break the Mosaic Law, but Gallio told them he was not interested in their internal squabbles. It must have shaped Paul's conviction that his enemies were his fellow Jews rather than the Romans.

After working for about eighteen months in Corinth, Paul, Aquila and Prisca went to Ephesus. Paul left them there to continue their apostolate while he travelled and preached, meeting opposition from some pagans, Jews who refused his message, and ultra-conservative Jewish Christians who considered all provisions of the Law still binding. Aquila and Prisca were still in Ephesus, where Christians met in their house, when Paul wrote from that city to the Christian community of Corinth in 57. They probably left in the middle of the year, as Paul did, because of anti-Christian riots.

Aquila and Prisca must have returned to Rome, because Paul sent greetings to them, through the deaconess Phoebe, and to "the church in their house". He greeted twenty-five people, several of whom, like Aquila and Prisca, had been in the East. Six of the names are Latin, the remainder Greek, but Grecian-sounding names were sometimes adopted by Romans. Several are those of slaves or freed slaves.

He greeted "those who belong to the family of Aristo-
bulus", who was probably a grandson of Herod the Great
living in Rome, and "those in the Lord who belong to the
family of Narcissus". This could have been the same
Narcissus, an upright freedman, who was a close collaborator of the Emperor Claudius. Among others he names are
"Andronicus and Junias, my kinsmen and my fellow
prisoners . . . men of note among the apostles, and . . . in
Christ before me"; Rufus, "eminent in the Lord, also his
mother and mine" (she had seemed a mother to Paul too);
and Urbanus, "our fellow worker in Christ".

Probably Paul wanted them to vouch for him. He was in a
delicate situation. To understand it, one has to go back to
Antioch some years before when Paul accused Peter of not
respecting the true meaning of the Good News. They had
clashed over the thorny issue of the right attitude to the
Law. In the first flush of his call, received on the road to
Damascus, to be apostle to the Gentiles, Paul took the
radical stance that "a man is not justified through works of
the law but by faith in Jesus Christ". Gentiles were of equal
status with Jews, and the whole Jewish tradition was in
jeopardy. For some Christian Jews, this was the equivalent
of permitting the Gentiles to seize their God. They had a
range of views, from those who insisted pagan converts had
to be circumcised to those who suggested it was advisable
for them to observe Jewish dietary laws and customs. The
underlying debate was whether Christianity was a separate,
though related, faith or a messianic renewal sect of Judaism.
Paul was convinced that a new intervention of God had
revealed truths which were not simply part of the Jews'
traditional religion.

Impetuous Paul continued his missionary journeys but
there was a danger that the churches he founded would be
detached from those which saw Jesus as the completion of

the Law rather than its negation. He isolated himself still further by a letter to the Galatians in which he passionately exalted Christ by downgrading the Law.

Usually Paul wrote only to churches he had founded, reproving or encouraging them. But he dedicated to the church in Rome, which he lauded to the skies, one of his most carefully crafted letters, which is more nuanced on Christ-Law relations than the epistle to the Galatians. Probably he wanted to create a good impression in Rome itself, but also in Jerusalem, where he was taking money he had collected, before visiting the imperial capital. It suggests that in the question of the relationship between Christianity and the Law, converts did not have to be circumcised but should not unnecessarily flout dietary and other provisions of the laws. In other words, the letter tells something about the church in Rome as well as about Paul.

It also hints that Gentile converts, as well as ultra-conservatve Jewish Christians, could be troublemakers. Using the analogy of a graft to an olive tree, Paul reminds the uppity Gentiles that "if some of the branches were broken off, and you, a wild olive shoot, were grafted in their place to share the richness of the olive tree, do not boast over the branches . . ., remember it is not you that support the root, but the root that supports you" (Romans 11:18). He warned against people who used pious arguments to confound the faith the Christians in Rome had received, and he recommended obedience to government authorities. "I long to see you, that I may impart to you some spiritual gift to strengthen you", he wrote, "that is, that we may be mutually encouraged by each other's faith". He looks forward to stopping in Rome on his way to Spain to "be refreshed in your company". He did come to Rome. But it took longer than he had anticipated, and the circumstances also were different – he arrived as a prisoner in chains.

On his way to Jerusalem, with money he had collected for the church there, he was denounced by Jewish leaders in Palestine ("we have found this man a pestilent fellow"). But Paul insisted on his right as a Roman citizen to be tried in the capital. Accompanied by a centurion named Julius, he was shipwrecked off Malta, where he spent three months. Eventually he landed in Puteoli (now Pozzuoli), near Naples, whose Christian community welcomed him. Christians from Rome came down the road a piece, about fifty kilometres along the Appian Way, to greet him as is recounted in the Acts of the Apostles which records, laconically, "And so we came to Rome".

Later portraits of Paul, which were probably based on memory rather than being merely conventional, show him as thin-faced, with a Semitic nose, a bald crown, and pointy brown beard. While awaiting trial in Rome, Paul was under house arrest. He was in his own lodging with a soldier as guard but was able to continue his ministry of teaching and preaching.

Three days after his arrival in the capital, he called together the city's leading Jews, told them he had arrived under arrest, and concluded that "it is because of the hope of Israel that I am bound with this chain". Although the Christians in Rome knew who Paul was and what he had been doing, the Jewish leaders did not. They were keen to hear his story and his opinion on Christians, "for with regard to this sect," they said, "we know that everywhere it is spoken against".

A whole day was put aside in which Paul presented his case "trying to persuade them about Jesus, arguing from the law of Moses and the prophets. He did not convince them all. As they went out into the Roman night, Paul, disappointed once more, quoted Isaiah to them:

. . . You shall indeed hear but never understand,
and you shall indeed see but never perceive.
For this people's heart has grown dull,
and their ears are heavy of hearing,
and their eyes they have closed,
lest they should perceive with their eyes,
and hear with their ears,
and understand with their heart,
and turn for me to hear them.

To top it off, Paul said that "this salvation of God has been sent to the Gentiles; they will listen."

The Acts of the Apostles concludes: "He lived there two whole years at his own expense, and welcomed all who came to him, preaching the kingdom of God and teaching about the Lord Jesus Christ quite openly and unhindered".

But it was not the end of Paul's story. In 63, after two years of house arrest, he was released, perhaps because no charge was laid against him. It was another plus for Rome and its justice. He set out again to spread the seeds of salvation, some say in Spain, others in Greece. He was arrested once more, but this time prison in Rome was harsher. And the great fire that destroyed Nero's Rome increased hostility towards Christians.

4

PETER AND PAUL

AUGUSTUS seemed to have solved most of Rome's problems, but among those he bequeathed to successors was the crucial one of succession. Although formally Rome was still a republic ruled by the Senate, in fact each emperor chose a successor or was replaced by whoever killed him. In most cases the Senate meekly approved.

It has been said of the Julio-Claudian emperors that "an arch-dissembler was succeeded by a madman, and a fool by a monster": Tiberius, Augustus's stepson, by Caligula, and Claudius by Nero. Dying emperors had a knack of ignoring worthy kinsmen in favour of unsuitable candidates, as did Claudius – who preferred Nero, Agrippina's son by a previous marriage, to his own son Britannicus. Agrippina then lost no time in poisoning Claudius, while Nero disposed of Britannicus.

Nero has become a symbol for depravity and cruelty. Peter he fixed to a cross and Paul he slew, so it is not surprising that Christians saw him as a prefiguration of the Antichrist. But many pagans also considered him a monster of impiety, a synonym for abominations, and he became a butt for contemporary pasquinades such as: "Alcaemon, Orestes and Nero are brothers, Why? Because all of them murdered their mothers".

Yet, after coming to power at the age of only seventeen, he ruled for five years with moderation. The credit probably goes to his mentor, the old, asthmatic Spanish Stoic Seneca.

This philosopher, who derided Roman religion, preached austerity although he himself was notorious for accumulating wealth, partly through usury. "Do as I say, not as I do" was his implied message. For some time Nero followed Seneca's elevated precepts but later had him put to death.

Hostile Suetonius has left a terse description of Nero:

Height: average
Body: pustular and malodorous
Hair: light blond
Features: pretty rather than handsome
Eyes: blue and rather weak
Neck: squat
Belly: protuberant
Legs: spindly

Unlike his warrior predecessors, Nero saw himself as an artist. Avid for applause, he entered poetry and song contests and then hung on the judge's verdict. Moreoever, he was capable of killing those, such as Lucan, who beat him. But there is something touching in his last words as he waited, quaking, for the death blow from enraged enemies who had pursued him to a villa on the Via Salaria: "What a great artist Rome loses!" He was thirty-one years old.

The deterioration in Nero's behaviour came rapidly as he killed his mother and exiled his first wife in order to marry Poppea Sabina. After the death of pregnant Poppea, allegedly because he kicked her in the stomach, bereft Nero married a male youth who resembled her, which prompted Romans to express regret that Nero's father had not contracted a similar marriage.

Nero may have found justification for his behaviour from friends such as Gaius Petronius, an ex-governor of Bithynia who became the young emperor's master of revels (eventually Nero had him killed) and is presumed to be the

same Petronius who wrote the racy novel *Satyricon*.
Petronius seems to have been a proponent of immoral chic.
Tacitus wrote that after his governorship, the refined
voluptuary Petronius "reverted to a life of vice (or of
apparent vice)". This helped him enter the circle of Nero's
intimates as a trend-setter or arbiter of taste (*arbiter
elegantiae*).

Tacitus's suggestion that "apparent vice" was Petronius's
best recommendation to Nero is a reminder of his contrast
between the Romans and the Germans, where "no one
laughs at vice, nor calls mutual corruption fashionable". It
also calls to mind Suetonius's comment on Nero: ". . . he
was convinced that nobody could remain chaste or pure in
any part of his body, but that most people concealed their
secret vices; hence, if anyone confessed to obscene practices,
Nero forgave him all his other crimes".

Satyricon is a window into a world where homosexuality,
sexual orgies and gluttony abound. The text is fragmentary,
the homosexual narrator is probably a literary device, and
the author is, or pretends to be, detached from his material.
Even allowing for these factors, what a distance there is
between Petronius and his contemporary in Rome, Paul of
Tarsus, who condemned ". . . men [who] gave up natural
relations with women and were consumed with passion for
one another, men committing shameless acts with men
and receiving in their own persons the due penalty for their
error" (Romans 1:27).

Paul seems to have made yet another missionary trip after
release from his two years' house arrest in Rome. But he was
arrested again and once more imprisoned in Rome. It was
his ultimate prison: tradition has it that Paul walked the last
of thousands of miles of Roman road at Tre Fontane (Three
Fountains), some three miles west of the city centre. As a
Roman citizen he had a right to decapitation outside the city

walls. The name Three Fountains derives from the springs which are supposed to have gushed forth at the spots where his head bounced. Within the church built on the spot, there are now shrines at descending levels to mark where the springs are said to have emerged. Paul was buried nearby, where St Paul's Outside-the-Walls was to rise.

Paul was a victim of the purge against Christians following the fire which destroyed most of Rome in midsummer of AD 64. Fanned by strong winds, it lasted almost a week, destroying ten of the city's fourteen quarters.

Nero was at his seaside villa in Anzio when the fire broke out. On hearing of it, he reputedly sang about the destruction of Troy, which was believed to have led to the founding of Rome. As it was known that he wanted to rebuild the overcrowded city centre as Neropolis, rumour was that his agents had spread the fire. If so, perhaps he was inspired by the Britons' Queen Boadicea, who shortly before had set fire to London. If not, the rumour indicates either that Romans thought their eccentric emperor capable of burning the capital or that his senatorial enemies simply took the occasion to discredit him. This seems likely, for Nero competently organized relief for the fire victims and instituted the first fire-fighting squads. He built a better-planned city, including his huge Golden House, of which a few remains still stand, near where the fire started.

But scapegoats had to be found, and Nero hit upon the Christian sect, whose members lived mainly in poorer quarters untouched by the fire, such as Trastevere and the urban tract of the Appian Way. As many Jews inhabited these quarters, it shows that by the mid-60s Roman authorities could distinguish between the two religions even though a good proportion of Christians must have still been ethnically Jewish. Describing these events almost half a century later, Tacitus uses a phrase which can mean either that humanity hated Christians or that Christians hated humanity; the first interpretation is in line with the Jewish leaders' comment on the sect to Paul when he first arrived in the capital: ". . . with regard to this sect we know that everywhere it is spoken against".

Perhaps Nero thought he could crush Christianity just as his stepfather Claudius had suppressed Druidic religion in Britain. Probably in Nero's time, as later, there was animosity towards Christians because they absented themselves from pagan ceremonies, which won them a reputation as impious; there were hair-raising stories about their adoring a man who had been crucified as a condemned criminal; and bloodcurdling accounts of rites in which they ate flesh and drank blood. Perhaps most damning of all at that moment were reports that Christians expected the world to end by fire.

Apparently the first Christians arrested denounced others until, in Tacitus' words, "a multitude was taken", which suggests that the Christian community was numerous. Writing in Rome three decades later, Clement said that Paul had been the victim of "zealous envy". This had been Paul's charge against archconservative Jewish Christians who had opposed him, but it could also have been a reference to orthodox Jews: they may have convinced Nero's wife, Poppea, to prompt action against a man they considered to be undermining their people's faith and their community's stability.

No reliable figures are available about the number of those killed, nor are the precise charges against them known. Were they killed as arsonists or because of "their name" – that is, for being Christians?

Nero opened his chariot racecourse-gardens at the Vatican for the prompt dispatch of the scapegoats, which was probably considered expiation to the gods for the fire. Usually such occasions included chariot races, humans pitted against wild animals, and theatrical, literary and musical performances.

Nero may have been an artist manqué, but as a sadist he was genuinely accomplished. He added several new twists to the spectacle, which was to have crucifixions as its high point. Criminals were sometimes burnt to death, but Nero used Christians covered with burning pitch as torches for the night games. In a mock hunt, he substituted animal prey with Christians in animal skins who were torn to pieces by enraged, famished beasts. Christians also seem to have substituted actors in enactments of legends which entailed their death. Perhaps Nero thought such strong fare would increase his popularity with Romans. He fancied himself as a charioteer as well as a singer-poet, and drove a chariot around the three-hundred-yard track.

Tradition has it that Peter was crucified, upside down at his own request, near the obelisk which had been brought to Rome from Egypt by Caligula less than thirty years before. In the sixteenth century it was shifted a short distance to its present site in the centre of St Peter's Square; it is the only thing still extant in this zone that Peter would have seen.

Portraits of Peter show him as round-faced, with short-cropped, slightly curled, greying hair and beard. But he is a less distinct figure than Paul. "Nothing can be determined", the biblical scholar D. W. O'Connor has written, about when Peter "came to Rome, how long he stayed, or what function or leadership, if any, he exercised within the Roman church."

His moderate views are well attested. The date and place of composition, the purpose and even the authorship of many apostolic-era writings are disputed. But it is widely thought that while the second Letter of Peter was written by one of his followers in the second century and not in Rome, the first Letter ("Peter, an apostle of Jesus Christ, to the exiles of the Dispersion . . .") was written in Rome either by Peter or a close collaborator before his death – and that it reflects his attitudes. Peter, or his collaborator, uses Jewish cultic language copiously, calling Christians "a chosen race, a royal priesthood, a holy nation, God's own people" (1 Peter 2:9). He recommends respect for civil authority: "Honour the emperor", for "by doing right you should put to silence the ignorance of foolish men"; apparently he was wary of criticism of Christians as disloyal, but his recommenation may have echoed ironically for him during his last hours in Nero's gardens. He takes for granted a two-tier church structure of presbyters or elders and younger men who are probably deacons. The fisherman-apostle appears as a shepherd concerned with stability and order in a church analogous with the home. The nomad-preacher was coming to terms with a settled community. With Christians meeting in houses used as churches, home and church were virtually identical.

There are layers of legend about Peter in Rome: that he spent his last weeks in the Tullianum, caverns that became the still-extant Mamertine prison on the Capitoline hill; that he lived with Senator Pudens, whose daughters, Pudentiana and Praxed, later had churches dedicated to them which can still be visited; that he bested the evil magician Simon Magus; that he had a daughter, St Petronilla; that as he fled Rome he had a vision of Christ entering the city and asked him, "*Domine, quo vadis?* [Where goest thou, Lord?]"

A fourth-century Roman sarcophagus in the National Archaeological Museum of Madrid shows Peter and Paul being sentenced by Nero. The scene sculpted probably did not take place, but it asserts partnership between the two apostles who earlier in Antioch had clashed sharply. Its message is that the apostles who had converged on Rome converged in the city. Was it partly because of the city's influence on them? Its grandeur might have given them a broader perspective on their task, and its Christian community may have helped reconcile their divergent viewpoints. However divided in life, they were united by their martyrdom and in the Romans' commemoration of them. The coupling of them in later references and representations was important for the prestige of the church of Rome.

The mother church was in Jerusalem, while the third city of the empire, Antioch, was the first centre for the diffusion of Christianity to Gentiles. But the martyrdoms of Peter and Paul gave a new status to the church of Rome. And within a few years of their death, Jerusalem was to be destroyed.

5

THAT OL' TIME RELIGION

NERO'S persecution occurred in a city which accommodated scores of religions: first-century Rome was a spiritual supermarket. There had been previous religious repressions, such as banishment of Jews or destruction of the temple of Serapis, but Rome was religiously tolerant. Respect for public order seemed to be the main criterion for the Committee of Fifteen which decided whether or not to admit new cults.

Before engaging an enemy in battle, Romans offered their gods a temple and games in their honour in Rome – in other words, a better deal than the gods received in their hometown. But Rome itself was conquered by the Greeks: increasingly the Roman pantheon became identified with the gods of Olympus, for instance Jupiter or Jove, king of the gods, with Zeus, and Minerva with Athena. At the same time, a cultural cringe towards more sophisticated Greece undermined simple trust in gods. Many of those who adopted Greek scepticism thought, however, that belief in gods was socially useful opium for the plebs, the common people.

The ranks of the gods were not reduced by the spread of scepticism. Besides the major gods, there were also minor genii to ensure fortune in various activities or to protect households, not to mention the foreign gods who increasingly took abode in Rome. "One was more likely to meet a god than a human", wrote Petronius, mocking this plethora of deities. Pagan Rome was anything but irreligious. Indeed, most Romans seemed ready to believe anything and everything. They often adhered to several different cults at the same time.

The strong point of Roman religion was its respect for tradition – or what was believed to be tradition when Augustus restored religion. Its most attractive aspect was a poetic, pantheistic sensibility, reflected in its tendency to personify everything. The reverse of the coin was that in the half-light of paganism all gods were grey, all equally true and false. This suited the military-political complex, for only a religion which claimed to know the truth could judge it. Because of the fuzziness, tricksters had a field day.

Their preferred venues were the sites of oracles, some of whom were reputedly inspired more by Bacchus than by Apollo. The popularity of oracles reflects the fact that places, rather than people, were considered holy.

Roman religion was concerned with the State's success rather than individuals' salvation. It was designed to ensure the peace of heaven, the gods' benevolence, for they could ensure victories but also be vindictive. Tolerance was based ultimately on fear of revenge, such as earthquake, plague, flood or war, from gods excluded or offended. Meticulous ritual was the way to get on the right side of capricious gods. If a mistake was made, the ritual was often recommenced as if it were an unknown language being repeated by rote. The officiants were state officials, magistrates who were performing a task, just as they would alternatively lead army units or appear in court. Consequently they came exclusively from the higher social classes.

Religion was pragmatic – a matter of doing something for the gods so that they would do favours in return. It did not entail doctrine or orthodoxy; nor was it a guardian of morality or an ethical code. Jupiter deposed his father, killed one of his grandsons, and married his sister. If gods transgressed, surely Romans could cavort. With due allowance made, gods were somewhat like saints – approachable intermediaries, and the more the merrier. Ancient Romans believed they needed all the help they could get. However, while saints fought their defects, gods gave their desires free rein. Somewhat like 1950s film stars and 1980s rock stars, they were allowed to do what was prohibited to ordinary mortals. If gods could not cut loose, but instead followed reason, they might as well have been philosophers leading virtuous lives.

Some conceived philosophy not only as knowledge but as a way to lead a good life and prepare for a good death. It performed functions, such as the search for meaning, now often identified with religion. Philosophers in Rome suffered for their convictions, as had their model and inspiration Socrates. Under Nero, a nephew of Augustus was "suicided" after being accused of Stoicism, while two other Stoics were exiled. Figures such as Seneca made Stoicism influential in Rome. Its ideal was indifference to everything but a worthy life and death. It stressed virtue, duty and reponsibility. Its god was not a roisterer but an abstract being beyond events and accidents. Stoics tolerated traditional religion as an allegorical representation suitable for the unenlightened.

Followers of Epicurus did not believe, as did the Stoics, that virtue was its own reward. Instead, they wanted virtue to result in happiness and pleasure. Placing a high value on friendship, they considered traditional religion as a system based on fear of the gods, of death and of its aftermath. As these fears thwarted happiness, they had to be scotched – particularly because to Epicureans the soul was only a chance congeries of atoms. Considered atheists by many, they in fact believed in superhuman beings untouched by human concerns.

Stoics tended to smug pride, and Epicureans to hedonism. But not all Romans sought sense in syllogisms. Mystery religions had more emotional appeal than moral philosophy, and with the conquest of an empire achieved, more Romans had time to ask what the point of life was.

The Middle East not only had older civilizations than Rome, but it also had more seductive religions, which spoke to souls rather than considering people solely as citizens. In 206 BC the Sybilline books kept in the Capitol, containing venerable oracles, advised the introduction of the Phrygian cult of Cybele. Installation in the Forum of the black stone symbolizing the goddess opened the way, despite the Senate's objection, to other Middle Eastern gods. Initially these temples and their priests were confined to the Forum, but with the arrival of businessmen, slaves, and craftsmen from the Middle East, the cults were practised throughout the city, and attracted Rome's religious "impulse buyers".

The Egyptian gods Isis and Serapis had several temples, and there were many followers for Cybele and Attis, while troops returning to Rome in the last years of the Republic had brought with them the Persian sun god Mithras. Traditional religion did not have to be abandoned to accept the mystery cults: it was a case of and-and-and rather than either/or. The only limit was ability to pay for entry to the cults. (Conversion in the Christian sense was an unfamiliar concept.)

Mystery cults were seen as a path to individual salvation. The adherents were a saved élite who did not need to strive for moral rectitude. The cults celebrated the death and resurrection of mythic figures in correspondence with nature cycles. Their rites packed a punch. Initiates stood beneath animals being sacrificed and were washed by their blood. Their processions were spectacular: in the rites of Attis, flagellant, castrated priests whipped themselves into ecstasy. For some Romans, bored by more restrained traditions, it was a welcome change of pace, but others saw the introduction of Hittite, Mesopotamian, Assyrian and what-have-you gods as degrading.

However, the mystery cults could inspire genuine religious sentiments, as shown by the novel *The Golden Ass*, whose lawyer-author Lucius Apuleius (AD 124–?) claimed to be a priest of Isis and, indeed, of all the gods.

Mithraism differed from other mystery cults because it emphasized morality, particularly loyalty, fidelity and obedience. It expected even tradespeople to be honest. Mithras was a god who brought the world salvation (life and fertility). The cult's ritual had some resemblance to that of Christianity: bread, wine and water were used in an *agape* meal for initiates who expected to ascend to heaven.

The Mithraic ethical code appealed particularly to soldiers, who took the cult from Asia Minor to the empire's borders, for instance on the Danube and at Hadrian's Wall, where a mithraeum can still be visited. In Rome, Mithraism arrived about 67 BC and later it was favoured by emperors such as Commodus and Diocletian. In the third century there were seventeen mithraea in the port Ostia and fifty in Rome itself, but most would not have held more than a hundred worshippers. For a time the cult seems to have competed with Christianity, but Mithras was a legend while Christ was a historical figure; moreover, it was disadvantaged because it excluded women. In Rome, Mithraism did not survive beyond the fourth century.

In addition to these cults, there were various forms of popular beliefs such a astrology, patronized by several emperors; magic, which likewise had imperial sanction; and, as already mentioned, oracles. There was a renowned oracle at Pareneste, now Palestrina, forty-two kilometres south of Rome.

Judaism and Christianity differed from traditional Roman religion, from moral philosophies such as Stoicism, and from most mystery cults. For one thing, they were monotheistic, and their God was a jealous god; for another, they imposed moral imperatives.

Judaism made converts, but they had to renounce their nationality, submit to circumcision, and then receive all the duties but not all the rights of ethnic Jews. Although Jews, who never forgot their former independence, were troublesome for the Romans, they had been granted exemption from Rome's civil religion and, moreover, were allowed to send money to support the Temple in Jerusalem.

Christians, however, had no sanction from tradition or ethnicity. Romans distrusted them as a new-fangled sect. For some, they had denied the Jewish god, and for others they were yet another degrading mystery cult in which cannibalism, incest and other abominations were reportedly practised. Romans had heard of men who became gods, but not of a God who became man – and then died a criminal's death!

Nevertheless, some Romans responded to the Good News from Palestine. It did not speak of a mythic figure but of a God-man who had been crucified under Pontius Pilate, had risen from the dead, and was now awaiting his faithful in heaven. The Good News was that God had taken the initiative and moved towards men. It was a shift from mythology to history.

The message that God is love, which now sounds banal, was a startling contrast to the pagan assumption that divinity was identified with power, whether in places, person or things. Jesus Christ was not God because of his power but because of his love. He was not above suffering and death but triumphed through suffering and death, undergone for the love of mankind.

Acceptance of the message was not stemmed by Nero's persecution, but for most Romans the city's irresistible rise to power was confirmation of their gods' validity. Moreover within a few years of Nero's mayhem, Rome achieved a memorable victory over the jealous God. Why change a winning game?

6

A DOUBLE
TRIUMPH

ROME had not seen anything like it for sixty years: not just one triumphal procession – the first-century equivalent of a ticker-tape reception – but two combined. The triumphal procession granted to Vespasian, who had begun the war against rebellious Jews, was combined with one granted to his thirty-year-old son Titus, who had completed it. In the meantime, Vespasian, at the age of sixty, had been proclaimed emperor by his troops.

Despite more than a century as a Roman protectorate, Palestine remained a troublesome province, and in 66 a rebel government had been established in Jerusalem. Nero, who was travelling in Greece, appointed Vespasian and his son Titus to restore order. Rome did not want trouble in the hinge zone between Egypt and Syria, but what Romans thought would be a mere border skirmish turned into a protracted war. The main reason was the civil war which followed Nero's death. The highly-motivated Jews' guerrilla-war tactics embarrassed the Romans, who excelled in face-to-face conflicts. But the Jews were isolated and could not resist when Rome brought its full force to bear.

The conflated celebration for Vespasian and Titus was designed to prove that Rome had achieved a great victory when it was, instead, a belated one. But Romans enjoyed triumphal processions which were accompanied by largesse in corn and money. For the occasion, temple façades were cleaned, incense was burned on their altars, and statues were garlanded. The Senate consulted the people's representatives before granting permission to hold a triumphal procession. But neither Senate nor people could say no to Vespasian.

Nero's attacks on the aristocracy and Senate had weakened them to the advantage of the army and the provinces, which supplied most succeeding emperors. Vespasian was the result of Nero's policies. He was the first non-noble emperor and came from a tax-collecting, landowning family of Rieti province, sixty kilometres north-east of the capital.

Vespasian had a strong face and broad forehead, but Suetonius claimed he always looked "as if straining to piss". This may be why one of his measures as emperor was to introduce public toilets and fine those who did not use them. "*Vespasiano*" is still Italian for a public toilet.

Vespasian laughed at a flunky who wanted to prove he descended from Hercules. The Army was his father and mother: he knew lineage was less important than battalions, and that the empire had been conquered by Italian yeomen-peasants rather than by Roman aristocrats, however divine their antecedents.

During the autumn night of AD 70 which preceded the triumphal procession, companies of the soldiers who had fought in the Jewish campaigns took up position near a temple of Isis outside the city walls. Vespasian, with chubby-faced Titus and his second son, nineteen-year-old Domitian, who looked a weaker version of his father, spent the night nearby. In the morning they appeared, wearing purple silk garments and laurel crowns, leading the troops, who had thunderbolts representing Zeus on their shields, through cheering onlookers into the city. At Octavia's portico the Senate, knights and other dignitaries awaited them. Vespasian and Titus sat on ivory chairs there, and the troops gave them an ovation which ceased only when the emperor held up his hand for silence.

Vespasian rose, partly covering his head with his robe, and prayed. Titus followed suit. Vespasian then made a mercifully short speech and sent the troops off to eat. The official party ate also, changed clothes, and sacrificed to the god before initiating the triumphal procession, which wound through various theatres to enable the greatest number of spectators to enjoy it.

It was a dramatization of Rome's might. Trumpeters preceded images of the gods who had ensured Rome's victories, wild animals from the war zone, and wagons with four-storey-high tableaux, often on carpets of gold. The towering tableaux, many surmounted by representations of how the commander of a vanquished city had been captured, depicted war episodes – cities laid waste, enemies, slain, defence walls breached, temples and houses in ruins, countrysides devastated.

Fettered prisoners of war, former enemies marching now to Roman tunes, filed past. Some onlookers pelted them with rotten vegetables. Seven hundred of the tallest and most handsome Jews captured in Jerusalem had been chosen for this humiliation, including the Jewish general Simon.

The spoils included even ships and, to the Roman Jews' consternation, treasures from the Jerusalem Temple: the heavy golden table, the seven-branched golden candlestick, and last but not least, the sacred book of the Law, the Torah: Rome's gods had triumphed over the God of the Jews.

The procession, with men bearing gold and ivory images of Victory at its rear, finally reached the huge temple of Jupiter on the Capitoline hill. Its progress had been so slow that at one point, Suetonius recounts, Vespasian said,

"What an old fool I was to demand it [the triumphal procession] as if I owed this honour to my ancestors or had even made it one of my ambitions! Serves me right!"

Vespasian, Titus and Domitian stood still and silent outside the temple, as was the custom of ancient Romans awaiting news that the enemy's general had been slain. They they heard the crowd roar triumphantly. It meant the Jewish general Simon, who had been dragged by rope through the Forum, had been killed.

The priests of the temple pole-axed an ox whose horns were gilded to indicate it was sacrificial. Vespasian must have been relieved that he could now enjoy a banquet. This may have inspired him to decide on the spot to build a temple to Peace in which the Jerusalem temple's treasure would be stored "as ensigns of this glory". The victorious troops ate on the town and afterwards probably painted it red.

The description of the triumph, scenes of which are sculpted on the Forum's Arch of Titus (built later to commemorate the occasion), is mainly based on an account by a Jew who won favour with the Romans: Flavius Josephus (37–101). Before he was nineteen he had been a Pharisee, Sadducee and Essene. He had spent three years in the desert with an Essene hermit before becoming a Pharisee. At the age of twenty-nine he came from Jerusalem to Rome to plead for the release of some arrested Jewish priests. Thanks partly to Nero's pro-Jewish wife Poppea, his mission was successful. That was in 64, the year of the Great Fire of Rome. Three years later Josephus unsuccessfully organized the defence of a Palestinian town against Vespasian. Josephus was captured but shrewdly forecast that the victorious Roman general would become emperor. His forecast was fulfilled two years later. When the Romans conquered Jerusalem, Josephus was with them and used his influence to save the lives of many compatriots.

Josephus accompanied Titus to Rome, where the emperor whose election he had forecast gave him a fine home. Assuming the name Flavius (which was that of Vespasian's family), this survivor set to work writing history and autobiography. He did not turn a hair at the slaughter of his compatriot Simon in the Vespasian-Titus triumph.

Josephus's career was exceptional, but it indicated that Rome's Jewish war did not lead to genocide or punitive measures, apart from fiscal ones, against Jews elsewhere. And in Titus's booty was Berenice, a Jewish princess whom he had wanted to marry but instead made his mistress. Berenice, who was one of the royal Herodian family, had as second husband her uncle, as third the king of Pontus and Cilicia, and then, for a quarter of a century, lived incestuously, it seems, with her brother Herod Agrippa II.

"Agrippa and Berenice came with great pomp", the Acts of the Apostles recounts, when Paul of Tarsus was held in Caesarea. Paul said he considered himself fortunate that he could put his case to Agrippa. "In a short time," Agrippa had said after listening to Paul, "you think to make me a Christian!"

Berenice, who had heard Paul in Caesarea, was now in Rome, where both those who had heeded the apostle and those who remained true to their Jewish faith were affected by the fall of Jerusalem and the Temple's destruction. It reinforced the idea of Rome as a hostile pagan power. For the city's Jews it must have been humiliating to see the Temple's sacred vessels and scrolls of the law as Roman trophies. Christians, whether Jewish or not, must have regretted the destruction of their mother church. But some Christians looked on Jerusalem's destruction as punishment for what the Jews of the city, or at least their leaders, had done to

Christ. Doubtless some would have pointed out that Christ had foreseen the Temple's destruction, which foreshadowed the world's end.

To rub salt into Jewish wounds, the tax which formerly went to the Jerusalem Temple was now destined to the Temple of the Capitoline Jupiter. There is an account of a man being forced to lift his toga in public to determine whether he was liable to pay. Tax collectors must have distinguished between Jews and Christians, and this tax would have been a factor in increasing the distance between them. Jews of the Diaspora tended to close ranks following the Temple's destruction, particularly as Jewish Christians had fled Jerusalem during the conflict. With the loss of their religious centre, they felt a greater need to define themselves and excluded those Jews who went to synagogues but also to house churches.

The nineteen-year-old Domitian, who had accompanied his father and Titus in their triumphal procession, was not given any part in government, and retired to his villa in the hills twenty-five kilometres south-east of Rome, devoting himself to literary studies. Jewish prisoners of war, who had worked on the Flavian amphitheatre (the Colosseum), were employed in building the villa. It is now part of the papal villa at Castel Gandolfo.

When Domitian succeeded Titus in AD 81, he ruled sternly but without cruelty for a decade. (There is an intriguing story of his summoning Christ's kinsfolk from Palestine for interrogation; finding them poor and humble, it was said, he sent them home.) Then, like Nero and others, he changed rapidly for the worse. These emperors probably heard footsteps behind them. Domitian became tyrannical after he found army generals plotting against him. The more threatened he felt, the more pretentious he became, insisting on being addressed as "Lord and Master" – his father,

Vespasian, would have laughed scornfully or sadly at such a title.

In a smite-before-being-smitten policy, Domitian struck out wildly. Many died for their political or philosophical beliefs or simply by imperial caprice; Christian martyrs must have gone almost unnoticed. The Consul Acilius Glabrio was condemned to death for "atheism", as was another Consult, Flavius Clemens, a cousin of the emperor. (Christians who rejected pagan gods were often accused of atheism.) Flavius Clemens's wife Flavia Domitilla, grand-daughter of Vespasian, was a Christian, according to the historian Eusebius. She was banished. Her sons Domitian the Younger and Vespasian the Younger seem to have been Christian and, as Domitian had no heirs, should have succeeded him.

However, there was no Flavian successor, for eventually, in 96, Domitian was killed in a palace revolt. For long periods, the Roman empire was a tyranny tempered by assassination. Some scholars claim the Apocalypse, thought to be written in the 90s, refers to Domitian's persecution when it talks of the sufferings of those who would not bear the mark of the Beast (the Emperor) on their foreheads.

7

THE ROMAN
ACCENT

THE three decades before the mid-90s had seen momentous events for the Christian community in Rome: the death of Peter and Paul, two periods of persecution, and the destruction of Jerusalem. Nero's persecution may have been simply due to a search for scapegoats after the fire which destroyed Rome, and Domitian's was apparently part of a paranoia involving other than Christians, but they could have shaken the young community, particularly as some of its members had denounced others. The community faced a further, internal problem: now that the mother Church had been destroyed and the apostolic generation was ending, what was the source of authority?

An answer was given loud and clear in unmistakably Roman tones by Clement. Reputedly consecrated by Peter, Clement is thought to have lived in a house near the newly-completed Colosseum where the church which bears his name now stands. His name suggests he may have been a freed slave of Titus Flavius Clemens who, as mentioned, was executed under Domitian: freed slaves often took the name of the owner who had granted manumission.

Since Clement wrote on behalf of the Roman Church, presumably he was spokesman for the college of presbyters which exercised collegial leadership. The letter, carried to the "church residing in Corinth" by two Gentile Christians who were probably freedmen, was occasioned by the deposition of certain presbyters, apparently by those claiming prophetic inspiration.

Clement argued vigorously for reinstatement of the presbyters, who, he claimed, enjoyed succession to the apostles by appointment. He deplored the "odious and unholy breach of unity" which "a few hot-headed and unruly individuals have inflamed to such a pitch that your [the Church of Corinth's] venerable and illustrious name ... has been brought into serious disrepute.

"Have we not all the same God and the same Christ?" he asked. "Is not the spirit of grace shed upon us all? . . . Brethren, be contentious and zealous for the things which lead to salvation!"

Clement justified the presbyters' rights both through apostolic succession and the natural order exemplified by Roman civil authority. Despite the fact that Claudius had expelled Jewish leaders from Rome, Caligula had wanted to put his own statue in the Jerusalem Temple, Nero had persecuted Christians as had Domitian, and Titus had destroyed the Temple, the spokesman for the Judeo-Christian tradition still spoke admiringly of the Roman imperial system. In the post-apostolic age, it was his model for a solid church structure as for effective evangelization.

Even though the Apocalypse compares the Roman emperor to the Beast seated on Satan's throne, Clement advised: "Let us, then, serve as soldiers, my brothers, for each in his own orderly ranking executes the order of the emperor." (Early Christians often saw themselves as soldiers of Christ, which makes it possible that the name "pagan" they bestowed on those who were neither Jew nor Christian was used not in its commonest meaning – "rustic" (in the early centuries Christianity was predominantly an urban religion) – but as "civilian" in contrast to "soldier".

They also referred to themselves frequently as athletes. (Evidently they admired not only Roman discipline, which had its own mystique, but also the dedication of athletes in contests which still had religious connotations.)

Clement admonished the Corinthians authoritatively that "if anyone disobey the things which have been said by God through me, let them know that they will involve themselves in transgression and no small danger." Obedience is due "to what we have written through the Holy Spirit."

Rome had spoken. The tone is still recognizable, even if it might be confused at times with that of a Roman lawyer or sergeant major. But its claims were ultimately based on the Spirit's inspiration of the hierarchy, and on them as bearers of apostolic authority. As authority, according to Clement, was exercised in the Spirit, it could not be challenged by self-proclaimed charismatics. Clement had established the rights of succession for those who could not, as he did, claim direct apostolic contact. His letter was based on the assumption that the apostles had not founded isolated communities but churches fed from the same source, vivified by the same Spirit, and with a unity of belief and practice. It also staked a strong claim for Rome as an arbiter of what was proper.

8

THUMBS DOWN!

AS seven of the eleven emperors before Trajan had died violent deaths, Clement's admiration for the Roman empire may seem surprising. But despite the chronic inability to achieve smooth imperial succession, the empire grew. It reached its greatest expansion with Trajan (98–117), the first emperor from beyond Italy: he was born in what is now Spain, the son of a father who was to become governor of Syria. Trajan divinized him.

Trajan has the too-smooth image of the perfect ruler – indicated by the title the Senate conferred on him, "*Optimus Princeps*" – and irreprehensible father of a model family. After military service in Syria, Spain and Germany, he was adopted by Domitian's immediate successor, the Emperor Nerva (96–98); adoption was to solve the imperial-succession problem for eighty years.

As a provincial, Trajan was free of the intrigues of Rome; moreover, he had no trace of Domitian's megalomania. He proved an honest, efficient administrator. He introduced greater equity in the legal system, instituted welfare offices to help orphans and poor children, reduced taxes, and reinvigorated the economy. He was the archetypal emperor, leading armies to victory in central Europe and Asia Minor. Between 101 and 107 he crossed the Danube and cancelled the shame of Domitian's military fiasco in this zone by conquering Dacia, which corresponds roughly to present-day Romania. In Asia Minor he pushed beyond Augustus's frontier at the Euphrates, conquered Armenia, the

Parthians, some of the Arab peoples and, like Alexander the Great, reached the Persian Gulf. He was the only Roman emperor to see the Indian Ocean. He died in Asia Minor.

Trajan was a great builder, founding the port north of Rome called Civitavecchia and the baths of Trajan, whose remains can still be seen near the Colosseum. But the most remarkable of his constructions was the forum he built after slicing into the saddle between the Quirinal and Capitoline hills. The centrepiece of this most imposing of imperial forums was the still-extant soaring column whose vigorous bas-reliefs of about twenty-five hundred figures recount the conquest of Dacia. Trajan's ashes were in its base. The column is as high as the hill it replaced. Originally the column was surrounded by a marble colonnade leading to a hall, a library of Greek volumes and another of Latin, but now only what were once small shops remain.

Not only all roads led to Rome but also all sea routes bringing the world's riches: grain from Egypt, venison and timber from Gaul; dates from African oases, silk from China, cotton from India; silver, copper and lead from the Iberian peninsula; ivory from Mauretania, glass from Syria; incense from Arabia, and philosophers from Greece.

However, Rome's pre-eminence and wealth were accompanied by problems. Its population had grown to a million, a figure not reached again until 1930. It was by far the largest city in the ancient world, a megalopolis. The overwhelming majority of people lived in five- or six-storey apartment buildings which were often jerry-built and in constant danger of collapse or fire. Most apartments were expensive, poorly lit, and without heating, running water or sewage. Day and night, the narrow streets were noisy. Traffic was so dense that deliveries were made only at night, when wagons competed with the frequenters of inns in ruining home-bodies' sleep. The satirist Juvenal complained that Romans were condemned to insomnia, and also noted that "everything in Rome is expensive".

A third of the population were slaves, who in many cases were not treated harshly, while another third were dependent on public handouts. Slavery was bonded labour; often slaves were considered an extended family, but of course they were cruelly dependent on their owners. At the age of thirty slaves could be freed, and some became influential: emperors favoured freedmen-collaborators as they undermined the power of the "old money" Senate.

Petronius's description of Trimalchio's feast in *Satyricon* reveals the world of freedmen and slaves. Except for the supercilious narrator and his two friends, all participants in the banquet are wealthy freedmen, coarse and ignorant but with a rough humanity. Sensing the narrator's contempt, they become aggressive. It is a saga of ostentation and sycophancy towards the super-rich host Trimalchio. His relations with his slaves are playful, but there is an underlying threat that he can dispose of them at will.

Not surprisingly, there were complaints that it had been downhill all the way since the sturdy republican era which had prided itself on strict morality and spartan family life. There was nostalgia for a time when the man was the master of the house, stern but just with wife and children; divorce was shameful; women were fertile as well as faithful, and prepared plain but plentiful meals; families worshipped regularly and worked willingly. It was the ethic of the peasant society which had made Rome great and which had been reflected in Augustus's choice of homespun clothes.

Now, it was lamented, all had deteriorated: wives had acquired equal rights, were reluctant to have children, and could obtain consensual divorce with separation of property. Parents, who had once insisted on a rigorous upbringing for their children, now merely pampered them.

The once granite family was crumbling. Homosexuality, which would never produce new recruits for the army, was on the increase. Decadent peoples from the East were undermining Romans' virtues. The rot began with the sophisticated Greeks, but they had been followed by other corrupters from Asia Minor who obtained the best positions and introduced ever more perverse practices.

> "To speak my Mind," wrote Juvenal,
> "I hate, in Rome, a Grecian Town to find:
> To see the Scum of Greece transplanted here,
> Receiv'd like Gods, is what I cannot bear.
> Not Greeks alone, but Syrians here abound,
> Obscene Orontes [Syrian river], diving under Ground,
> Conveys its wealth to Tyber's hungry Shoars,
> And fattens Italy with foreign Whores."

The complaints of Juvenal and other nostalgics probably entailed a measure of cant, for they idealized a past in which the weakest had gone to the wall. But they showed that while Trajan was extending the empire, some feared that the empire had conquered Rome.

Immigrants were not the only problems from the provinces. In 114 Trajan received a lengthy letter from his close collaborator Pliny, who, at the age of fifty, after a legal and military career, had recently become governor of Bithynia on the Black Sea, in what is now Turkey. The governor was the nephew of the naturalist Pliny, who had died in AD 79, despite the protective cushion on his head, as he walked towards Vesuvius to observe at closer quarters the eruption which buried Pompeii. Pliny the Younger had likewise observed the Christian phenomenon with curiosity for he found them of both sexes, all ages and social classes, not only in the towns, but in villages and the countryside. Attendance at temples was down, as was the sale of sacrificial meat – bad news for both butchers and temple priests.

Pliny explained that he had condemned to death those who, under interrogation, had persisted "with inflexible obstinacy" to proclaim themselves Christians. He had then received an anonymous denunciation of many Christians but released those who denied the charge, venerated the gods and emperor, and cursed Christ. Others, who said they had ceased to be Christians, gave him an insight into the sect's practices: Pliny reported that Christians met and sang the praise of Christ "as if he were a god" and then swore to repay loans, and not to rob or commit adultery. Later on the same day they met again to eat "innocuous" food. Pliny's adjective seems a denial of the charge that Christians were cannibals. He decided to investigate further. He had two deaconesses arrested and tortured them: all he found was "squalid superstition". He decided to ask Trajan's advice because of the "great number of those accused". But he concluded optimistically that the rot could be stopped, claiming indeed that his measures were already having a positive effect: "It [the superstition] can be checked and cured. Certainly my statistics already show that temples, long left desolate, have begun to be thronged again, that religious ceremonies, long intermitted, are being renewed, and that there is again a market for the flesh of victims, for which till recently hardly a single buyer could be found. This all leads me to realize what a multitude of men can be reformed, if room is left for repentance."

Pliny's query was a tricky one for Trajan. Its subtext was: "I know it's customary to kill these Christians, but for the life of me, I can't see why. P.S.: If we keep pushing, we'll have everyone back in the temples." In his brief response, Trajan praised Pliny for investigating the cases of those denounced as Christians. "Indeed," he continued, "no general regulation can be given that would have anything like a clear-cut form. They [the Christians] are not to be sought out; if they are denounced and proved guilty, they must be punished – providing only this, than a man who denies that he is a Christian and proves it by his act, that is to say by praying to our gods, however suspect he may have been in the past, may now obtain forgiveness through repentance. Anonymous documents must not figure in any charge. That would be a vile precedent, not permissible in our age."

Later the Christian Tertullian criticized Trajan for saying that Christians were not to be sought (implying they were not criminals) but if found should be condemned (implying they were). Tertullian's concern was with the truth of the matter, whereas Trajan wanted to ensure smooth government.

This first-ever imperial pronouncement on the status of Christians shows that even though their behaviour was blameless, they were still liable to the death sentence. It also suggested there was unease and confusion about how to handle Christians.

Although Pliny promised that paganism could be restored, Trajan was not willing to run the risk of social disruption by ordering a purge of Christians. He implied that if Christians were discreet, they might survive; but discretion could fuel rumours about their unsavoury practices.

It was an ambiguous situation in which initiatives against Christians came from provincial governors. Consequently the Christians' standing varied from province to province, according to how sensitive governors were to pressure coming mainly from representatives of rival religions.

Trajan had shown himself anxious to wash his hands of the problems caused by Christians in the provinces. But there were Christians in Rome, too, who aroused hostility by quietly refusing to participate in pagan sacrifices or pagan games and spectacles which retained some of their original religious connotations.

The gladitorial contests, stadium games, chariot races and theatre shows were on a mind-boggling scale. In 108–109 Trajan celebrated his conquest of Dacia with games lasting 123 days during which 10,000 gladiators fought and 11,000 animals were killed. At the dedication of the Colosseum in AD 80, Emperor Titus gave games lasting 100 days in which women gladiators fought and there was a naval battle in an artificial lake.

Before the Colosseum was built, gladiatorial shows seem to have been held in the Forum itself. Probably they began as a means of honouring the dead, but in the empire they were more political theatre. Politicians staged them to win support. As citizens' opportunities to engage in politics diminished in the empire, shows, games and theatre provided the only occasions to confront their rulers. At times the crowd at the games expressed its disapproval of the emperor, who almost always attended and, with thumb up or down, exercised his right over life. A theatre crowd forced Tiberius to return a statue he had taken from the public baths, while an actor once derided Nero, who was thought to have poisoned his adoptive father (Claudius) and to have attempted to drown his mother, by accompanying the banal line "God bless father, God bless mother" with gestures of taking poisoned food and drowning.

Public killings were a Roman rite, followed enthusiastically by huge crowds. They were the playing fields of the empire, war on a domestic scale. Pliny said the frequent bloodbaths for the populace's amusement inspired contempt for death. However, it was the death of others, outcasts such as criminals and Christians. Or of animals.

Nero has been execrated for using Christians covered in pitch as torches in AD 64, but at least they had been accused of setting fire to the city. However, a spectator was once thrown to wild dogs merely because he had made a witty remark against Domitian, and when there was a shortage of condemned criminals, Caligula commanded that crowd members be thrown to wild beasts. Imperial caprice could go no further.

Africa and the courts of law were scoured for show fodder. Condemned criminals were sent from the provinces to fight to the death in Roman arenas. The search for gladiators – mostly prisoners, but some of them freedmen (including senators) or even women – was strenuous. It redounded to the credit of the politician who staged a show if he could present exotic animals such as tigers, elephants, crocodiles, giraffes, rhinoceroses, ostriches and hippopotami. In some single shows there were as many as six hundred lions. They tore criminals to pieces or killed one another. If necessary, they were stimulated by firebrands. Amid stage sets simulating scenery of their natural settings, any survivors were hunted and killed. Romans did not need zoos.

The arenas, racecourses and theatres could take more spectators than even their largest contemporary equivalents: the Circus Maximus, which is now an open field, measured 600 metres by 200 and could seat over 250,000, while the Colosseum, which could be covered, took 50,000. The covered theatre of Pompey seated 27,000 (today there is a restaurant in what used to be its foundations). On an average, big spectacles were staged two or three times a week. Some pagan Romans deplored the crassness of the shows, for instance the practice of killing real people in plays. Seneca described the light relief in the arena between the morning's wild-beast contest and the afternoon's gladiatorial show: "All the previous fighting had been merciful by comparison. Now finesse is put aside and we have pure, unadulterated murder . . . In the morning men are thrown to lions and bears. At midday they are thrown to the spectators themselves. No sooner has a man been killed [in fights between criminals], than they are shouting for him [the victor] to kill another, or to be killed. The final victor is kept for some other slaughter . . . You may object that the victims committed robbery or were murderers. So what? Even if they deserved to suffer, what is your compulsion to watch their sufferings? 'Kill him,' they shout, 'beat him, burn him. Why is he too timid to fight? Why is he so frightened to kill? Why so reluctant to die?' They have to whip him to make him accept his wounds."

Seneca disapproved of shows in which "men drank men's blood" but admitted they were a powerful drug. Watching them made him feel "more callous and less human".

Of course, Christians had profound objections to the contempt displayed to humans and the appeal made to animal instincts among the spectators. For them the person was holy, whereas pagans connected holiness with rites, temples or shrines. Needless to say, Christians were horrified to find fellow believers being used as choice items in the spectacles.

They also objected to the religious matrix of the shows, underlined by the fact that sometimes attendants were dressed as gods: slaves who, with a red-hot iron, tested whether victims were only feigning death were dressed as Mercury/Hermes, while those who dragged away the dead could be dressed as Dis/Pluto, the god of the underworld. Some Christians were led around the arena dressed as pagan priests or priestesses before being stripped naked and left to the mercy of the wild beasts.

It is not known if this treatment was reserved for Ignatius, who came from Antioch to Rome towards the end of Trajan's reign. Like Paul of Tarsus, he came as a prisoner ("chained to soldiers," he wrote, "who only grow worse in the face of kindness"). Unlike Paul, he knew he was to be martyred – and woe to anyone who tried to prevent it. Ignatius felt he had run a good race and the finishing tape was in sight.

Ignatius, who had known John the Apostle, was a key figure in a key city for early Christianity. Antioch, capital of the Roman province of Syria, was the first important urban centre of the Christian movement outside Jerusalem, and the site of the first organized circumcision-free mission to Gentiles. There, in the empire's third city after Rome and Alexandria, both Peter and Paul worked; Peter seems to have been the dominant figure in its Christian community for many years. Matthew probably wrote his gospel there around AD 80–90. It was in Antioch that those Jews elsewhere called "follower of the Nazarene" began to be called Christians (Acts 11:26). It was in Antioch that the Church was first called "Catholic" – by Ignatius, who had a precocious awareness that each particular Christian community was linked to all others in a Church most catholic or universal: "Wherever the bishop appears", he wrote, "let the people be there; just as wherever Jesus Christ is, there is the catholic Church."

It seems that in Rome a two-tier structure of presbyters and deacons prevailed until the end of the first century, but by early in the second Antioch had established a three-tier structure of bishop, a college of presbyters (elders), and a group of deacons. Everything depended on the bishop. He guaranteed the unity of faith; he filled roles which were formerly those of prophets and teachers, and authorized others for liturgical functions. It has been suggested that the emergence of the "monarchical" bishop was prompted by the need to oppose his authority, now that the apostolic age was ending, against those who claimed to be leaders because they were in receipt of private revelation.

It is not known exactly when Ignatius was arrested, nor when he was martyred in Rome, but it is thought to be about 110. He left an indelible record of his journey to death, or what Christians considered their heavenly birthday, in the letters he wrote on his way to the capital. He wrote to his confrere Polycarp, leader of the church in Smyrna, and to Christian communities in six cities.

A section of his letter to Polycarp is a striking example of the use of the military analogy for the Christian life: "Be pleasing to Him whose soldiers you are, and whose pay you receive. May none of you be found to be a deserter. Let your baptism be your armament; your faith, your helmet; your love, your spear; your endurance, your full suit of armour. Let your works be as your deposited withholdings, so that you may receive the back pay which has accrued to you."

He was on his way to collect his back pay by dying an atrocious death in the capital of the empire, but for him it was the seat of the most admirable of churches. His letter to the Roman Church provides valuable evidence on the martyrdom of Peter and Paul and their standing. After addressing it in glowing terms (". . . worthy of blessing, worthy of praise, worthy of success, worthy of sanctification, and, because you hold the presidency of love, named after Jesus Christ and named after the Father . . ."), he continued: "You have envied no one; but others you have taught. I desire only that what you have enjoined in your instructions may remain in force. Only pray for me that I may have strength both inward and outward; that I may not merely speak but have also the will; that I may not only be called a Christian but may also be found to be one . . .

"I am writing to all the churches, and I enjoin all, that I am dying willingly for God's sake, if only you do not prevent it. I beg of you, do not do me an untimely kindness. Allow me to be eaten by the beasts, which are my way of reaching God. I am God's wheat, and I am to be ground by the teeth of wild beasts, so that I may become the pure bread of Christ.

"Not as Peter and Paul did, do I command you. They were Apostles, and I am a convict. They were free, and I even to the present time am a slave. Yet, if I suffer, I shall be the freedman of Jesus Christ, and in Him I shall rise up free. Now in chains, I am learning to have no desires of my own.

"I have no taste for corruptible food, nor for the pleasures of this life. I desire the Bread of God, which is the flesh of Jesus Christ, who was of the seed of David; and for drink I desire His Blood, which is love incorruptible . . .

"By this short letter I beg you to believe me. Jesus Christ will make it clear to you that I am speaking the truth. He is the mouth which cannot lie, by which the Father has spoken truly.

"Remember in your prayers the Church in Syria, which now, in place of me, has God for its shepherd, Jesus Christ, along with your love, shall be its only bishop."

9

THE FIRST
HERETICS

TRAJAN adopted his cousin Publius Aelius Hadrianus (Hadrian), who came from the same Spanish town (Italica) and was his companion-in-arms, making him his successor. Forty when he became emperor, Hadrian was tall, with regular features but small facial scars which prompted him to grow a beard, setting an imperial fashion which lasted (with the exception of Heliogabalus) until Constantine. His secretary Suetonius had access to imperial archives and became the historian, or gossip columnist, of the Caesars, supplying spicy but often tendentious stories of their behaviour which contrasted with the decorum expected in Roman society. Hadrian believed in zero growth for the empire and even withdrew from Armenia and Persia. Part of his conservation policy was to build a wall across Britain to protect it from the barbarous inhabitants of Scotland.

In about 124 he received, from a proconsul in Asia Minor, a query similar to Pliny's regarding the appropriate attitude toward Christians. Hadrian's answer was similar to Pliny's; his main concern was to punish unjust accusers: "If someone makes a denunciation, by Jupiter, merely to calumniate, decide on the gravity of the case and give them the appropriate sentence."

Hadrian travelled constantly with a team of technical experts who planned and assigned public works. But he also travelled because of a lively curiosity. About the time he received the proconsul's query, he was presented with a defence of Christianity by a philosopher named Quadratus. Unfortunately, only a fragment remains. It marks an important development. Earlier Christian writing had been about events in Palestine, and accounts of the apostles' missions and their encouragement or admonitions to Christian communities. It was directed to Christians, but given the persistent ignorance about Christianity, something else was needed. Through its apologists, Christianity now began to present itself to pagan society.

A particularly eloquent example of the genre was the anonymous Letter to Diognetus. Some scholars claim it was part of Quadratus's "Apology" and that Diognetus was a pseudonym for Hadrian, but more of them date it to the mid-second century or even the end of it. It deserves partial quotation for its incisive antitheses: "The difference between Christians and the rest of men is neither in country, nor in language, nor in customs. They dwell in their own fatherlands, but as temporary inhabitants. They take part in all things as citizens, while enduring the hardships of foreigners. Every foreign place is their fatherland, and every fatherland is to them a foreign place. Like all others, they marry and beget children, but they do not expose their offspring. Their board they set for all, but not their bed. Their lot is cast in the flesh, but they do not live for the flesh. They pass their time on earth, but their citizenship is in heaven. They obey the established laws, and in their private lives they surpass the laws."

The letter defended by attacking, for it claimed the moral superiority of Christians and in a form which would appeal to connoisseurs of rhetoric: "They love all men, and by all are persecuted. They are unknown, and they are condemned. They are put to death, and they gain life. They are poor, but make many rich; they are destitute, but have abundance of everything. They are dishonoured, and in their dishonour they are made glorious . . . When they do good, they are punished as evildoers; and when they are punished, they rejoice as if brought to life. They are made war upon as foreigners by the Jews, and they are persecuted by the Greeks; and yet those who hate them are at a loss to state the cause of their hostility.

"To put it briefly, what the soul is to the body, that the Christians are to the world. The soul is spread through all parts of the body, and Christians through all the cities of the world. The soul dwells in the body, but it is not of the body; and Christians dwell in the world, though they are not of the world. The soul is invisible, but it is sheathed in a visible body.

"Christians are seen, for they are in the world; but their religion remains invisible."

Did it remain invisible to Hadrian, neither seen nor heard? It seems he did not respond to the Apologia of Quadratus. Perhaps its arguments were too peremptory or too simple for Hadrian, whose travels and renowned villa in Rome suggest an enjoyment of dizzying perspectives, of labyrinthine possibilities, of dabbling with gods rather than confronting God. While travelling in Egypt with his wife, Trajan's niece Sabina, the bisexual emperor became infatuated with Antinous, a beautiful youth from Bithynia. When Antinous drowned, Hadrian dedicated a city to him as well as statues, some in the form of a god, and temples.

After another Jewish revolt in 133–35, Hadrian excluded all Jews from Judea, and rebuilt Jerusalem as a pagan citadel named Aelia Capitolina after his family and the Capitol in Rome. At this stage, monotheism probably irritated Hadrian: it was a stop-sign in his realm of possibiliies, where divinity was a do-it-yourself affair. If

Antinous could become a god, so could Hadrian, but the monotheistic message was: "There's only one God, and he's not you."

In 134 Hadrian returned to Rome, where he rebuilt the Pantheon, and also built his villa and mausoleum. A mile from that of Augustus, which was used for the burial of emperors until Nerva, it was to be the imperial burial place for the next eighty years. In the Renaissance it was linked to the Vatican by a wall-passageway, now under repair. With additions, the mausoleum became the still-extant Castel Sant'Angelo. Perhaps a more curious memorial to Hadrian is the temple his successor Antonius built; it is still a temple, but of money, for it is the Rome Stock Exchange.

The mists surrounding the early Christian community in Rome are shown by the fact that its bishop Telesphorus was martyred either at the end of Hadrian's reign (117–138) or the beginning of that of his successor Antoninus (138–161), but nothing more is known about his reliably-attested death, and precious little about his life.

The mists veiling early Christianity clear up briefly in a book called *The Shepherd* to reveal a surprising and charming landscape. Its author, Hermas, was a slave sold by his owner to a Roman matron, Rhode, who became Christian. Hermas, a married man, "began to love Rhode as a sister". One day he helped her emerge after she had bathed in the Tiber and thought what a blessing it would be "if I had a wife of such beauty and stylishness". (He advised those tempted as he had been to think of their wives' charms, but he depicted his own as a shrew.)

Later, as a freedman, he recalled this scene with remorse while walking toward Cumae near Naples, where he had a farm before losing it through bad management. He fell into a trance during which an elderly lady appeared and told him he should be more worried about his shrewish wife, and his children who had apostasized, than about Rhode.

After prayer and fasting, Hermas had further visions which he recorded in *The Shepherd*, a text popular with early Christians, including eminent figures such as the third-century theologian Origen and the fourth-century historian Eusebius. One of its main themes was that forgiveness is possible even for those who sin after baptism. This was keenly debated, as some maintained the Church must consist of saints whereas others saw it composed also of sinners.

In his visions, Hermas was told that fasting must be accompanied by giving the poor what would otherwise be consumed and that the rich should support the poor who, in turn, should intercede for the souls of the rich.

Among the dangers Hermas warned against were involvement in business and property deals, which distract from holiness; quarrels, status-seeking, hatred, deceit, irascibility, licentiousness; faith without good works, self-appointed teachers, and false prophets. Among the many virtues he admired, the principal were faith, temperance, fortitude and patience while the defects he deplored were headed by unbelief, intemperance, disobedience and deceit. He lauded assistance to widows, visits to orphans and the poor, ransoming God's servants in their difficulties, showing hospitality, nonresistance to anyone, being of quiet disposition, being poorer than all men, honouring the aged, practising justice, exercising fraternal charity, enduring insult, abstaining from spite, comforting those who are troubled in spirit, not rejecting those who have stumbled in the faith but winning them back, calling sinners to order, and not oppressing debtors.

Although the outlook is thoroughly Christian, the pagan world is close at hand: Hermas presumed the old lady he met near Cumae was the pagan Sibyl (or prophetess) who resided there, but later was told he was mistaken: "While I slept, brethren," he recounted, "a revelation was made to me by a very handsome young man who said, 'Who do you think the old woman is from whom you received the book?' I said, 'The Sibyl.' 'You are wrong,' he said.

" 'Who is she, then?' I said. 'The Church', he replied.

" 'Why, then, is she old?'

" 'Because,' he replied, 'she was created the first of all things. It was for her sake that the world was established.' "

A further indication of the nearness of the pagan world is that the protagonist reaches Arcadia, which pagan poets had invented as a rural idyll. It is an appropriate setting for the revelation he receives, which recommends a return, through repentance to "guileless innocence". You are nearer to God in Arcadia, Hermas seems to suggest to his contemporaries, than anywhere else in the Roman world.

This master of the interior life stressed, not the contrast between Christian and pagan, but that between the country and the city, where Christians are exposed to all sorts of compromise. His allegory proposes a return to the undivided heart, to the innocence which enables him to kiss virgin girls and dance with them "as cheerfully as a child".

Hermas's light touch is a surprise. Persecution barely impinges on his gentle, joyous Arcadia. "All those who have suffered for His [Christ's] sake are glorious in God's sight and all their sins are remitted . . . but their fruits are different and . . . some of them surpass others. All who were tortured when called before the magistrates, but suffered with alacrity, are decidedly more glorious in the Lord's sight, and their fruit is superior. But those who were cowardly and lost in uncertainty, who debated in their hearts whether to deny or confess, yet finally suffered – the fruit of these persons is inferior, because the deliberation occurred to them."

Hermas's warning against status-seeking and business deals suggest that some Christians were all too well inserted in society. His counsels are provocative and stimulating, like his description of worthy bishops who are "friendly to strangers and receive the servants of God into their homes gladly, without sham. They have given shelter constantly by their own ministrations to the indigent and widows, and their conduct has always been pure. Therefore they will be given shelter by the Lord forever." The words acquire added piquancy if, as a contemporary document claims, he was the brother of Pius I (*circa* 142–155), who came from north Italy.

Pius was facing problems which could hardly be resolved by Hermas's "guileless innocence". Marcion, a strong-willed, enterprising native of Pontus on the Black Sea in what is now Turkey, was a major one. A shipowner, Marcion had run into trouble both with his fellow Christians in Pontus and with the redoubtable Bishop Polycarp of Smyrna. About 140 he came to Rome, where he made generous financial contributions to the Christian community and gained adherents for his teaching that the New Dispensation contradicted the Old, that the God of Jesus was quite different from the God of the Jews, a "barbarian" who favoured terrorists such as King David.

Marcion's insistence on the newness of Christ's revelation made him urge his follwers to break all social and familial restraints. For Marcion, martyrs attested to the new age in which death had been conquered; but those without the blessing of martyrdom could also testify to victory over death as celibate missionaries, for procreation was a link with death. Celibacy was a triumph

over the natural world, which had been superseded by
Christ.

For a time Christians in Rome saw Marcion as successor
to Paul of Tarsus. But when Paul was quoted effectively
against Marcion, he complained that the Pauline texts had
been altered. He established what he claimed were the
authentic Pauline texts as well as a biblical canon which
excluded the Old Testament and parts of the New
Testament writings.

This was an incentive for the Church to establish its
biblical canon. The Gospel of Mark is believed to have
been written in Rome by Peter's companion in the 60s,
while those of Matthew, Luke and John, written in Asia
Minor between the 70s and the end of the century, reached
Rome later. Several other gospels were written in the
second century but were not accepted into the canon.

In AD 146 Marcion was forced out of the Roman
Christian community, which had accepted his donations
but not, ultimately, his ideas. Undeterred, he returned to
Asia Minor and set up his own church with bishops and
presbyters. Marcionism spread rapidly within the empire
and beyond its eastern frontier through zealous groups of
celibates of both sexes. But Marcionites had counted their
chickens while refusing to hatch them. The movement
eventually died out, partly because replacement of dying
members had to come solely through conversions as there
were no families.

Marcion was a foretaste of the greater problems which
came with Gnosticism. For Christians now, "gnosticism"
has the pejorative connotaion of "heretical", but initially
many Christians were proud to claim to have the true
gnosis (knowledge). Gnostics were spiritual guides or
sages. Often they were not ordained.

Scholars do not agree as to whether Gnosticism was a

coherent system of belief before Christianity. There was a mishmash of philosophy and religion in Asia Minor at about the time Jesus Christ preached, and some Gnostics were apparently attracted to the new faith. Many Gnostics mixed Jewish traditions, Christian elements and pagan philosophical systems. Although it is tempting to say there were as many different kinds of Gnosticism as there were Gnostics, all had a markedly dualistic outlook which contrasted the spiritual to the material.

Gnostics who were Christians considered the material world had been created by a demiurge, identified by many with the sinister God of the Old Testament. In their view, Jesus Christ had come to deliver a message which could free man from entrapment in the material world so that his divine spark could reach the upper light. The Enlightened Ones were those who had the gnosis or information which would not only reveal this to men but also help them negotiate their way through the various levels of an intricate otherworld and ultimately attain liberation. They had the cosmic code words. Christian rites such as baptism, Gnostics claimed, hinted at these truths which could not be revealed to ordinary faithful who believed in sin, repentance, faith and good works. But those who were initiated into the arcane truths would be a saved élite. Gnosticism proclaimed the inside track as the way to salvation. For Gnostics, the only sin was ignorance. It was a religion for the clever who were silly enough to believe God would consider them worthier than other men.

Although the Gnostic cosmogony was bafflingly complex, its consequences were clear enough. Gnostics were fatalistic and profoundly suspicious of the natural world, of flesh, society and government. Some Christian Gnostics tolerated marriage, but considered the married second-class believers. In Gnosticism, being took on an unbearable lightness, whereas Christians melded body and soul, flesh and spirit. Gnosticism had something in common with the mystery cults, for it tended to evade history in favour of myth. It made Jesus Christ ethereal; it evaporated His humanity. For Gnostics, Jesus had come to deliver a message rather than winning redemption through suffering. Like the pagans, Gnostics could not credit that the Word had become flesh. Gnosticism was above suffering; Gnostics shunned martyrdom, as they considered the body unimportant.

A leading Gnostic guru named Valentinus, who came from Alexandria to Rome in 138 and taught there until 160, for a time won many followers attracted by what must have seemed a more intellectual and spiritual version of Christianity. His starting point was the insight of Paul of Tarsus, that with Christ's coming the whole universe was redeemed, but he went on to elaborate a symbolic system which eventually brought him into conflict with Roman Christians. They accused him of propounding a hybrid doctrine.

Christianity was not monolithic, and many of its beliefs had not been defined. There were different strands with different emphases: Levantine Christianity, with various attitudes to the Jewish heritage; Hellenistic Christianity, which absorbed part of the Greek philosophic tradition; and North African Christianity. There were messianic elements and domestic versions of the faith. All this made it difficult to discern whether teachings and practices were unsound or merely the product of different contexts. Prophet-teachers who were disapproved of in one community could be heeded in another. The problem of discernment was a constant one which became acute with Gnosticism, as some Christian Gnostics adopted parts of Platonism.

After a long, influential spell in Rome, Valentinus's welcome eventually ran out. Roman Christians rejected him for allegedly putting Christ on the same level as Plato and Pythagoras: if knowledge is the royal road to salvation, philsophers become kings.

Of course, history is written by winners, or at least they can destroy the losers' literature, as happened with most Gnostic writing. (Some of Valentinus's work, along with those of other Gnostics, was found at Nag Hammadi in Egypt in 1945–46.) But at the time many concluded that a better bet than Gnosticism's fuzzy and fragmented teaching was a core of doctrine and practice common to what was being called the Great Church which spread from Lyons to the Euphrates and beyond. Communications between one Christian community and another could take three months, and obviously the diverse communities took colouring from their contexts, though there was a recognizable identity. Or so thought Hegesippus, a convert Hellenistic Jew, who visited various centres of Christianity to gather information to combat Gnosticism. He recounted his journey about AD 180 in his *Memoirs*, where he affirmed that he found among the bishops in various cities on his way to Rome "a continuance of that which is proclaimed by the Law, the Prophets, and the Lord."

The Christian philosopher Justin in Rome, Bishop Clement of Alexandria, Bishop Irenaeus of Lyons, and the lawyer Tertullian in North Africa were among those who provided antidotes to Gnostic literature. In other words, the Church was laying it on the line. Probably no one could define Gnosticism – it was like trying to eat jelly with a fork. But the Church was prepared to define its own beliefs and establish a canon of Scripture.

The struggle against Gnosticism, like that with the Marcionists, brought bishops together, since those with claims to secret knowledge and private revelation not only undermined Scripture but also bishops' authority as the true teachers of apostolic tradition. The bishops and other defenders of the faith underlined that Jesus was the fulfilment of the Old Testament. They rejected the dis-continuities of the newborn Marcionite Christians and the instant salvation of the Gnostics. They did not identify Christianity with shrill radicalism opposed *a priori* to society, nor with pessimism about human affairs and the world of the flesh.

One of the most eminent of these bishops was Polycarp of Smyrna, whose trenchant style is evident in his letter to the Philippians: "Everyone who does not confess that Jesus Christ has come in the flesh is an Antichrist; whoever does not confess the testimony of the cross is of the devil; and whoever perverts the sayings of the Lord for his own desires, and says there is neither resurrection nor judge-ment, such a one is the firstborn of Satan. Let us, therefore, leave the foolishness and false teaching of the crowd, and turn back to the word which was delivered to us from the beginning."

Irenaeus said that Polycarp had called Marcion "first-born of Satan" to his face. "Recognize me, Polycarp!" Marcion said when he met the bishop. "I do recognize you", Polycarp responded. "I recognize the firstborn of Satan." Second bishop of Lyons, Irenaeus had been a pupil of Polycarp in his native Smyrna. Irenaeus lived until the beginning of the third century, a witness to the merits of Polycarp, who in turn had known the evangelist John: the apostolic influence lasted long and reached far.

Shortly after Anicetus (*circa* 155–166) became bishop of Rome, Polycarp visited the capital and tried to convince Anicetus to celebrate Easter, as in the East, on the day of Passover. But the church in Rome did not yet have any special Easter festival. Anicetus told the bishop from Smyrna that he would simply continue to celebrate the Lord's resurrection each Sunday. He invited Polycarp to celebrate the Eucharist with him, which shows that the rites they used were similar. They would have been helped by the fact that for both the ecclesiastical language was Greek.

On return to his port city, Polycarp was martyred. Because of the hostility of pagans and Jews, twelve Christians were thrown to the wild beasts in the amphi-theatre. They did not flinch, but when Quintus, a Christian visitor from Phrygia who had offered himself for martyr-dom, saw the wild animals at close quarters, he heeded the Roman proconsul's invitation to "offer sacrifices to the gods".

The crowd, which had enjoyed the killing of the twelve Christians, screamed for Polycarp's blood ("Death to the atheists! Go and get Polycarp!"). But the eighty-six-year-old bishop had left Smyrna and it was several days before police and calvary captured him. He was brought to the amphitheatre where the other Christians had died. The governor, who presumably was familiar with the rescripts of Trajan and Hadrian regarding Christians, told the old bishop that to save his life he would have to shout, "Death to the atheists!"

With lips almost closed, Polycarp repeated the formula. The governor insisted that Polycarp take an oath to the emperor and curse Christ before he could be freed.

"I've served Him for eighty years, and He has never done me wrong," responded Polycarp. "How can I blaspheme against my king and my saviour?"

The governor insisted that Polycarp swear by the emperor, but instead, the bishop offered to instruct the governor about Christianity. The governor advised the bishop to try to sway the crowd, who were evidently his main concern. Polycarp said, "The mob does not deserve a speech of defence".

He was burnt to death. The Christians, wrote an eyewitness, gathered Polycarp's bones, "more precious than the rarest jewels, of greater worth than the purest gold", to lay them in a suitable resting place and decided to gather yearly to celebrate the anniversary. It was the beginning of the cult of martyrs of the post-apostolic age (the practice did not spread to Rome for another sixty years). The description of Polycarp's trial is from the oldest hagiographic document, written because another Christian community in Asia Minor requested an account of the event. In Rome, too, there seemed a new awareness of the need to preserve the memory of the martyrs, because four or five years after Polycarp's burning, in about AD 160 while Anicetus was still bishop, the shrine to Peter was erected on Vatican hill.

The laborious Roman legal system facilitated dissemination of the martyrs' stories, rather as the cumbersome Italian system allowed Red Brigade terrorists ample time and opportunities to tell their very different stories through interviews given in court and in prison.

Whereas Ignatius of Antioch wrote seven letters on his way to martyrdom in Rome, other martyrs kept diaries in their cells. Eyewitnesses described martyrs' deaths. Christians transcribed proceedings from court records. Martyrs became heroes of the arenas to rival pagans' jockey-and-gladiator heroes. Their stories not only inspired some Christians but also challenged non-Christians. Later writers embellished many of these accounts, making too much of a good thing, but critical examination has shown the authenticity of a certain number.

10

NO JUSTICE
FOR JUSTIN

BEARDED Justin had travelled a long way, not only spatially but also intellectually, by the time he reached Rome. Born of Greek parents in what is now Nablus, Palestine, early in the second century, he had studied philosophy in Ephesus. He recounted that he began studying with a Stoic tutor who, however, admitted that he knew nothing of God. Justin decided therefore to attach himself to an Aristotelian, but left him when he requested payment. A Pythagorian was the next choice, but Justin felt he would waste too much time if he satisfied his new mentor's demand that he first learn music, astronomy and geometry. A Platonist gave more satisfaction, but finally, as Justin sat by the seashore, an old man disproved Platonic teaching on the soul and convinced him that the prophets had foretold Jesus Christ's coming.

The old man by the sea is probably an allegorical figure, but Justin became convinced that Christianity was "the true philosophy". Presumably wearing the customary philosopher's sari-like gown draped over one arm, with a shoulder left bare, he became an itinerant teacher.

Christianity was a historical revelation, not a philosophy, but it was important that Christian philosophers emerged. Cultured pagans tended to despise Christians as un-educated, partly because of the generally poor Greek of the New Testament. For their part, Christians tended to distrust philosophy because many of them associated it with paganism, and more particularly because some Gnostic heretics adopted a Platonist outlook, although there was a sharp difference between Gnostic depreciation of the material universe and Platonism's wonder at its beauty.

Justin, however, saw pagans as groping for the truth. He found seeds of truth in the Sybilline oracles. He considered Socrates a precursor of Christ in denouncing the falsity of pagan gods. He called Socrates, like Abraham, a Christian before Christ. Having saved Socrates, he could plead for his pupil Plato: the God of Plato, he claimed, was the God of the Bible. With Justin, Christianity's debate with pagan philosophy began in earnest.

Embarked on an ambitious project of appropriating pagan culture, Justin thought Hadrian's successor Antoninus could be convinced of Christianity, or at least informed about it to forestall further persecution. Antoninus, a tall, wealthy, migraine-suffering aristocrat of Gallic origin, was a stay-at-home as much as Hadrian had been a wanderer. He did not go farther from Rome than his seaside villa, twenty-five kilometres away at Lavinium. He was a generous and sagacious ruler, the nearest to an emperor-saint. The Senate gave him the title "Pius".

Justin addressed a defence (or apology) of the Christian faith to the emperor, "guardian of justice, philosopher . . . and lover of learning". In the appendix, Justin recounted the story of a Christian who convinced a woman to abandon dissolute ways but was denounced for this by her husband. The Christian was condemned by the Roman judge Urbicus, which provoked an onlooker, Lucius, to shout: "Why condemn this man, who is not guilty of adultery, fornication, murder, theft of any other crime, but only of confessing himself a Christian? Your sentence,

1. Figure said to be St Peter depicted as the Good Shepherd, in a fragment of a fourth-century frieze in the St Sebastian Catacomb.

2. An inscription from the cover over the burial site of St Paul in the Basilica of St Paul's-Outside-the-Walls.

3. The Graffiti wall in the crypt of St Peter's in the Vatican. In a niche inside the wall the bones were found which some claim are St Peter's.

4. A mural fresco showing a Eucharistic Banquet in the Hall of the Sacraments in the St Callistus Catacomb.

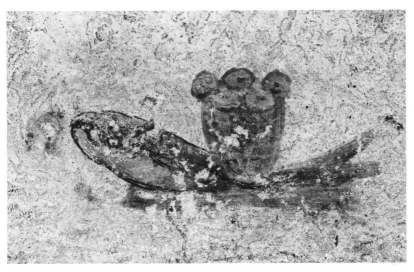

5. Fish with bread and wine, representing the Eucharistic Christ, from the Crypt of Lucina.

6. The third-century Crypt of the Popes is the most venerated site in the St Callistus Catacomb. The six bishops of Rome buried here are Pontian, Anterus, Fabian, Lucius, Sixtus II, and Eutychian. All were saints.

7. The dove as a symbol of peace, from a marble slab in the St Callistus Catacomb.

8. A peace symbol appears also on the tombstone of Irene (also shown on the cover).

9. A gallery in the St Callistus Catacomb, showing the *loculi* or cavities gouged in soft tufa stone in which the Christians buried their dead.

10. Saints Cornelius and Cyprian, third-century heroes depicted in a sixth-century fresco from the Crypt of Lucina in the St Callistus Catacomb.

11. Detail of a crypt in the St Callistus Catacomb.

12. A medallion frieze from the recently restored Arch of Constantine in Rome, showing the Emperor leaving Milan to advance on Rome, the Battle of the Milvian Bridge, and Constantine, surrounded by senators, addressing a crowd in the Forum.

Urbicus, is unworthy of Antoninus Pius, the heir of Caesar and friend of wisdom; unworthy, in the last analysis, of the holy Senate."

There was no need to draw diagrams for Urbicus. He condemned Lucius to death, and also another spectator who followed his example. As far as is known, this story and the apology as a whole had no effect on Antoninus Pius, but the anecdote showed that defence of Christianity was a risky undertaking, as Justin was to learn at first hand.

He left Rome but returned when Marcus Aurelius (161–180) succeeded his uncle Antoninus Pius, whose daughter Faustina he had married. For a philosopher such as Justin, it may have seemed that the Platonic ideal of a philosopher-king was to be fulfilled. Marcus, thin-faced, with protuberant eyes and spouty nose, was a Stoic with a taste for the ascetic: for instance, from the age of twelve he had always slept on the floor. He found the empire he had inherited beset with problems.

There was unrest along the Danube, in Britain and on the eastern frontier. Once Hadrian had halted Rome's expansion, pressure was felt on the empire's borders. The army lost the habit of fighting and winning. Tribes crossing the Danube reached northern Italy in 166, when a terrible epidemic raged in Rome itself. Its victims coughed convulsively, were sore-ridden, and had pestilential breath: the bubonic plague had been brought to the capital by troops returning from fighting the Parthians. As if this were not enough, the Tiber flooded. "If the Tiber floods, if the Nile drops," the Christian polemicist Tertullian was to write later, "the cry goes up, 'The Christians to the lion'." The calamities probably contributed to the increase of hostility against Christians, whose absence from the ceremonies of propitiation ordered by the emperor caused resentment. Christians were accused of not pulling their weight for the imperilled empire.

Marcus Aurelius proved an adroit, courageous military commander, driving the invaders back to the Danube. Between spells of fighting the barbarian Quadi, sitting in his camp at Vindobona (Vienna) where he followed a vegetarian diet because of a stomach ulcer, Marcus Aurelius reflected on things human and divine in terms which would have been familiar to Justin.

His *Meditations* have an unassuming but elevated tone: "Be careful not to affect the monarch too much or to be too deeply dyed with the purple, for this can well happen. Keep yourself simple, good, pure, serious and unassuming; the friend of justice and goodness; kindly, affectionate and resolute in your devotion to duty. Strive your hardest to be always such a man as philosophy would have you be. Reverence the gods, succour your fellow mortals. . . ."

He has wide horizons: "My own nature is a rational and civic one: I have a city, and I have a country: as Marcus I have Rome, and as a human being I have the universe; and, consequently, what is beneficial to these communities is the sole good for me."

His ideals are exalted. The good man, he specifies, is distinguished by "his refusal to soil the divinity seated in his breast . . . and in his resolve to keep in serenity and decorous obedience to God, admitting no disloyalty to truth in his speech or to justice in his actions."

The virtues he admires are industriousness, modesty, sobriety, dignity, prudence, justice, temperance, fortitude, self-control, self-respect, unselfishness and obedience to the divine will. "Nothing can be good for man," he was convinced, "unless it helps make him just, self-disciplined, courageous and independent."

So far, so high-minded; indeed, Marcus Aurelius was

positively stratospheric. He represented morality without spirituality, duty without joy. He was worthy but morose, an example of immaculate dejection. His soulscape mirrored the level, grey Danubian marshes where he campaigned.

The courageous commander could retire to his tent to reflect: "A spider is proud of catching a fly; so is one man of trapping a hare or another of netting a sprat; or a third of capturing bears or Samartians [Danubian tribesmen]. If you go into the question of principles, are these anything but robbers one and all?"

Such detachment has an admirable aspect, but it also seems that of the last star in a dying universe. With a sidereal eye, Marcus Aurelius describes the whole earth as "no more than the puniest dot", which matches his collectivist outlook ("What is no good for the swarm is no good for the bee") and an overwhelming sense of the transience of human affairs.

Marcus "sees through" life, which he calls "an empty pageant". "My purple robe", he reflects, "is sheep's wool stained with a little gore from a shellfish; copulation is friction of the members and an ejaculatory discharge . . ." "When a thing's credentials seem most plausible," he advises, "lay it bare, observe its triviality, and strip it of the cloak of verbiage which dignifies it."

Marcus Aurelius can seem the Emperor of Boredom: did he miss anything at all during his years on the frontier? "As the performances in the circus or in other places of entertainment tire one with their perpetual repetition of the same sights . . . so it is with the whole experience of life . . . all things prove to be ever the same. How long, then . . .?"

The world-weariness is profound: he sums up life as "yesterday a drop of semen, tomorrow a handful of . . .

ashes." The note is repeated until it becomes a dirge mixed with disgust: after describing the difficulties of living, he comments: "In all this murk and mire, then, in all this ceaseless flow of being and time, of changes imposed and changes subdued, I can think of nothing that is worth prizing or pursuing seriously." What, he asks, do the public baths bring to mind? "Oil, sweat, dirt, greasy water and everything that is disgusting. Such, then, is life in all its parts, and such is every material thing in it."

He does not believe in the possibility of the new and, as if fearful of delusion, counsels himself against impulse. This inhibition produces surprising reflections such as the emperor reminding himself not to be angry with those who have body odour or bad breath.

"Never allow yourself to be swept off your feet", he warns himself. But this, of course, was what had happened to Paul of Tarsus (at least he is traditionally depicted as being swept off his horse) and, even if in slow motion as he trudged from one philosophic school to another, to Justin. Marcus Aurelius's rejection of enthusiasm was a crucial difference in what was to be a long-distance clash with Justin.

This becomes clear in Marcus Aurelius's comment in praise of those prepared for death, which includes a sideswipe against Christians: ". . . preparedness, however, must be the outcome of its own decision; a decision not prompted by contumacy, as with Christians, but formed with deliberation and gravity and, if it is to be convincing for others, with an absence of all heroics."

In a sense, the whole trick for Marcus Aurelius was to remain indifferent to suffering, to keep a stiff upper lip, not deigning to notice it. He could not approve Christians' embracing it as the fast track to salvation – nor, it can be deduced, a God who took flesh and suffered. For many

Stoics, God was a perfectly rounded whole, immune from accident or event.

Marcus Aurelius was prepared to withdraw from life at any time by suicide. He did not object so much to Christians (as he saw it) killing themselves, but to the fact that they acted without decorum in the arena or in law courts. It may have been inconceivable for him that Christians affirmed their beliefs in law courts although threatened with dire punishment. In the back of the minds of Stoics such as Marcus Aurelius, there probably lurked the teaching of Seneca's father, who wrote a book of exemplary legal cases which argued that those who confessed without torture and condemned themselves must be mad. The word the emperor used to describe Christian behaviour in court – "contumacy" – suggests insubordination, the stubborn refusal to obey a legitimate order. Perhaps his hostile opinion was partly due also to reports of heretical Christians (Montanists) who sought martyrdom.

Nevertheless, Justin had confidence in Marcus Aurelius, or at least addressed a plea for Christians to him as he had done with his predecessor. Doubtless Justin could underwrite many of the emperor's affirmations, such as : "Nothing human can be done without reference to the divine", and "Dig within. There lies the well-spring of good; ever dig and it will ever flow."

In his second spell in the capital, Justin lodged with a certain Martin above Timiotinus's baths. Christians came to him to discuss the faith. It was the first Christian school in Rome, or perhaps it would be more accurate to call it a study circle. Justin also resumed his dialogue or polemics with non-Christian philosophers. One was Crescens, a Cynic. Cynics usually advocated a simple life, but Justin found Crescens pompous. It seems that Crescens denounced Justin and his disciples to the civil authorities, although it is not clear, as so often is the case with early Christians, what the charges were. It caused the trial, under a philosopher-emperor, of a philosopher at the instigation of another philosopher before a judge with philosophical training. The year was probably AD 165. According to the "Acts of the Martyrs", Justine was tried before the prefect Junius Rusticus together with his fellow Christians Evelpistus, who was one of the emperor's slaves; Hierax, whose parents were from Asia Minor (Phrygia); plus Chariton, Paeon, Charito and Liberian. These six met in Justin's lodgings to discuss their faith.

Interrogated by Junius Rusticus, Justin's companions proclaimed they were Christian. Evelpistus, who said his parents were Christians from Cappadocia, responded, "I am Christian also, liberated by Christ, and by this grace share the same hopes as my companions."

On Junius Rusticus's prompting, Justin gave an account of his faith: he said he was willing to suffer for Jesus Christ as it would mean he would be saved. When Justin and the others refused to sacrifice to the gods, Junius Rusticus ordered that they be beheaded.

How could a harmless philosopher be killed judicially, along with his companions, under a philosopher-emperor? Or Christians be sadistically tortured and killed a decade later in Lyons, where some were forced to sit nude on scalding metal chairs? One was a Roman citizen whose status was referred to the emperor without its being any aid to him.

Perhaps Marcus Aurelius, busy among the Germanic Quadi, was not personally involved in such cases. But there is another possibility. Junius Rusticus, who judged Justin and his companions, had been Marcus Aurelius's Stoic professor and law tutor. The emperor began his

Meditations by counting his blessings (the fifth was that he kept away from the racetrack). The seventh blessing was Junius Rusticus, who had taught him "to avoid rhetoric, poetry and verbal conceits, affectations of dress at home, and other lapses of taste . . . If any others, after falling out with me in a moment of temper, showed signs of wanting to make peace again, I was to be ready to meet them at once halfway."

Marcus Aurelius also gave thanks for having had as an early tutor Cornelius Fronto, a celebrated orator and rhetorician. "To my mentor Fronto", wrote Marcus Aurelius, "I owe the realization that malice, craftiness and duplicity are the concomitants of absolute power; and that our patrician families tend for the most part to be lacking in the feelings of ordinary humanity."

Yet in public speeches Fronto showed malice against Christians. As Minucius Felix, a Christian laywer who later reproved Fronto, said, "He spattered abuse like an agitator."

Fronto repeated the canard that Christians, after drunken banquets, engaged in lustful embraces and incest in the dark. Such slander might have been inspired by the behaviour of heretical sects. But Fronto was in a position to obtain sound information and not merely to retail popular prejudice.

Junius Rusticus did show some interest in Justin's beliefs at his trial, but it seems that, like Fronto, he was part of an élite too smug, too stiff-necked, to have made a leap of sympathy which would have enabled them to understand people whom they considered alien. Marcus Aurelius was shaped by such "Brahmins". It seems that he could tolerate anything but what he considered unseemly fanaticism. The gulf between the philosopher-emperor and the philosopher Justin was wider than the Christian imagined.

Justin was convinced that God calls even the body to resurrection, whereas Marcus Aurelius felt it was due for either "extinction or transmutation". If his was transmuted into a Stoic heaven which communicates with the Christian one, doubtless Marcus Aurelius and Justin still have endless philosophical discussions. Justin could be forgiven for wryly quoting the emperor's fine phrase "Tolerance is a part of justice".

11

A CHRISTIAN COUNTERCULTURE

ALTHOUGH temperament as well as convictions must have contributed to Marcus Aurelius's world-weariness, family fortunes may have been an additional factor. Two of his four children died young, a daughter married unhappily, and the fourth child was his successor Commodus, who could not have been more different from his philosopher-father. Marcus Aurelius wrote appreciatively of his wife Faustina, but Romans gossiped that she was promiscuous. This may have been merely an attempt to find an explanation for Commodus, who, rumour claimed, was fathered by a gladiator.

Powerfully built, with curly beard and hair, Commodus, who was nineteen years old when he became emperor, fought over seven hundred battles in the amphitheatre. He charged the treasury heavily for each appearance, but he put on quite a show: he dressed in a lion's skin, and his hair was sprinkled with gold dust. In one two-day blood feast with spear and bow, he killed five hippos, two elephants, a rhinoceros and a giraffe. One morning, from safe walkways constructed specially across the arena, with exactly one hundred spears he killed one hundred lions and bears. A contemporary writer commented that it proved "accuracy rather than courage".

Eventually Commodus installed a reign of terror, but he was not personally hostile to Christians. Yet there were martyrs in his reign. One of them, Apollonius, articulated a fundamental aspect of the Christian attitude to martyrdom. Brought before the prefect Tigidius Perennius, Apollonius was threatened with death when he refused to sacrifice to gods and emperors but responded nonchalantly that dysentery or fever could just as well kill him. Perennius accused him of wanting to die.

It is worth noting that a Stoic such as Marcus Aurelius affirmed that a man should be ready to "withdraw" from life. He had little love for it but was choosy about the style of his going forth. The high Roman manner was to open one's wrist veins in a hot bath.

Responding to Tigidius Perennius, however, Apollonius reaffirmed his love of life. "I enjoy living," he affirmed, "but I don't fear death because I love life; the only thing more precious than life is the eternal life of the immortal soul who has lived well in this world."

Perennius admitted that he did not know what Apollonius was talking about. There was much mutual misunderstanding when Christians were tried by pagan judges, who sometimes pleaded with them to be reasonable or flexible so that they could be freed. Judges did not intend to create martyrs but wished to win people back to the traditional religion. (This ignored the fact that some families had been Christian for many generations.) The judges were used to people who could venerate the Roman gods as well as their own, whether Attis, Serapis, Mithras or what-have-you. The Christians' refusal to sacrifice, then, must have seemed obduracy which amounted to rebellion – or madness.

Christians themselves had divergent attitudes toward martyrdom. Ignatius of Antioch seemed keen to race into the lion's mouth, whereas police had to find Polycarp of Smyrna before he could be martyred.

It was difficult to find an approach which eschewed both provocation and compromise, which found the mean between a sellout and a showy suicide. To seek suffering was unhealthy, but acceptance of it could give it meaning; gradually the conviction arose that the test was not whether one tried to avoid capture but how one faced the trial of martyrdom.

The problem became more acute with the emergence of the New Prophecy Movement, also called Montanism from its founder Montanus, who encouraged Christians to welcome martyrdom. It was probably one reason why the pagan polemicist Celsus considered Christians subversives.

Born in Phrygia, which corresponds roughly to present-day Anatolia (Turkey), Montanus claimed that he, together with two women companions, had the gift of prophecy. Their message was that as Christ was about to return, Christians should fast more rigorously, avoid marriage, reject commerce with pagans or their State, and welcome martyrdom. "You'd better believe it", was Montanists' advice to fellow Christians, for to do otherwise would be rejection of the Holy Spirit. The movement spread rapidly, splitting many communities and worrying, among others, Bishop Irenaeus of Lyons, a large proportion of whose faithful came from Asia Minor. In 177 Irenaeus wrote an anxious letter about Montanism to Bishop Eleutherius of Rome, but he did nothing.

The pagan élite constantly reproved Christians for the prominence they gave to the poor and ignorant; Christianity was vulgar. Abolition of social distinctions was perhaps the community's most striking feature; right from the beginning it attracted slaves but also leading citizens. It cut across cultural assumptions, too, by allowing the humble to proselytize. "In private houses nowadays," Celsus complained, "we see wool workers, cobblers, laundry workers and the most illiterate rustics who get hold of children and silly women in private and give out most astonishing statements, saying that they must not listen to their fathers or schoolteachers, but must obey them. They alone know the right [Christian] way to live."

Temporarily Rome had solved the problem of imperial succession, but the past deification and dumping of emperors must have induced many people to put their trust elsewhere.

Reinstatement of those killed, exiled or censured during one reign could be rapid, but then just as rapidly reversed. As Tacitus drily remarked: "The happiest day after the fall of a tyrant is the first." Emperor Galba staged an elaborate ceremony after the killing of Nero to rehabilitate his (pagan) victims, but within a year he and his two successors had died violent deaths. Contemporary Eastern European experience shows that violent and rapid political reversals push some to seek an unchanging God. For Romans, Christians represented a counter-culture in this as in other ways. In the capital of ostentatious wealth and insensate bloodshed, Christians refused to participate in gargantuan spectacles. This brought them abuse as spoilsports, but it must also have meant recognition as an alternative. One reliable acknowledgement of the Christians' distinctive lifestyle came from the satirist Lucian of Samosata. Born in Asia Minor (Commagene in Syria), Lucian was a barrister and literature teacher who worked in Athens, Rome and Gaul. His public readings of his literary works were popular.

Lucian distrusted all forms of religious belief, for he considered that Epicurus had liberated men from superstition. He made wicked fun of charlatan oracles (such as The World Prophecy Champion), exposing not only religious tricksters but also the gullibility of their fans. For Lucian, polytheism was a heavenly protection racket.

It is noteworthy that in *Alexander*, his sketch lampooning The World Prophecy Champion, Lucian bracketed Christians with atheists as nonbelievers in divinities. Alexander invites a mob to attack them: "he produced an oracle declaring that Pontus was full of atheists and Christians who had most wickedly blasphemed against him, and must be stoned and driven out of the land."

Lucian's *On the Death of Peregrinus Proteus* portrays a swindler, Peregrinus Proteus, who became a bishop but was then imprisoned by the governor of Syria. His faithful raised a substantial sum for the swindler which enabled him to buy his release and still declare a profit.

Lucian had only the haziest idea who Christ was and what He meant to His followers, but most of his audience would not have known more. As a result, his backhanded compliment to Christians as generous although gullible is particularly convincing. After saying Christians came from other communities throughout Asia Minor to help Peregrinus, he commented: "They are always incredibly quick off the mark when one of them gets into trouble like this: in fact, they ignore their own interests completely. Why, they actually sent him [Peregrinus] large sums of money by way of compensation for his imprisonment, so that he made a considerable profit out of them! For the poor souls have persuaded themselves that they are immortal and will live for ever. As a result, they think nothing of death, and most of them are perfectly willing to sacrifice themselves. Besides, their first lawgiver persuaded them that once they stop believing in Greek gods and start worshipping that crucified sage of theirs, and living according to His laws, they are all one another's brothers and sisters. So taking this information on trust, without any guarantee of its truth, they think nothing else matters, believing in common ownership."

In the second half of the second century in Rome, Latin gradually replaced Greek as the Church's language. Previously Christians had spoken Latin but had prayed (and written) in Greek. The switch to the vernacular made Christians more at home in Rome, but it increased the likelihood of misunderstandings with the East, where the majority of Christians lived. East and West were no longer sure what each other were talking about – was *hypnostasis* the equivalent of *substantia*?

The use of Latin in Minucius Felix's book *Octavius* showed that, by about the beginning of the third century, some Christians were becoming more at home in Rome. *Octavius* carries the reader into the Roman world. It first scene is at the Roman seaside.

Although it is an early autumn morning in Rome's seaport Ostia, it is warm enough for the sea breeze to be welcome. Three lawyer friends have taken advantage of the law courts' recess for the grape harvest to have a day at the sea. As they stroll towards the beach, one of them, Caecilius, blows a kiss to the statue of the god Serapis; Ostia had temples to all the gods of the traders who frequented it.

Octavius, a convert to Christianity like the third lawyer Minucius Felix, reproves him for leaving Caecilius in ignorance and declares his contempt for all idols "however well-carved, anointed, and crowned with garlands".

The trio walk, paddling in the breaking waves, as Octavius, who has left his wife and children in his native North Africa while in Rome on business, regales his friends with stories of his sea voyage. Then they retrace their steps, observing blocked boats and boys skimming stones off the waves. Minucius Felix notes that Caecilius is sombre and finds that he is irritated by Octavius's accusation of ignorance. As Caecilius wants to debate the matter, they sit on rocks which form a breakwater, with Minucius Felix in the middle.

Minucius Felix's friendship with Octavius dated from the time they were law students. Participation in trials against Christians had convinced Octavius to convert, and Minucius Felix followed his example.

Octavius had returned to his native North Africa, while Minucius Felix practised as a lawyer in Rome, where he became a friend of Caecilius, who was another North African.

Minucius wrote his account of the trio's excursion to Ostia as a memorial to Octavius after hearing of his death. He recorded Caecilius's arguments against Christians as the lawyers sat on the Ostia seashore rocks but orated as if in court.

Caecilius argued that ignorant Christians could not arrive at truth, as it eluded even philosophers. The safest course, he advised, was to trust the gods who had made Rome great. He then made a violent attack on Christians' behaviour: they feed on human flesh and blood, kill newborn children, indulge in love-feast orgies, encourage incest, and worship a crucified malefactor. Christians must practice obscene rites – or otherwise, he asked, why would they operate in secrecy, without temples, altars or recognizable images? Caecilius also complained that Christians were spoilsports, absent from public rejoicing and ceremonial festivities, and carping critics of spectacles such as the theatre.

He called them "a gang . . . of discredited and proscribed desperadoes [banded] together against the gods. Fellows who gather illiterates from the dregs and credulous women, with the instability natural to their sex, and so organize a rabble of profane conspirators, leagued together by meetings at night, and ritual fasts and unnatural repasts, not for any sacred service but for an inexpiable crime – a furtive race which shuns the light, mute in the open but garrulous in corners. They despise the temples as if they were tombs; they abominate the gods, sneer at our sacred rites. Pitiable themselves, they pity (if this is possible) the priests; half-naked themselves, they spurn positions of honour and purple robes. What strange folly! What incredible insolence! They do not care about present tortures, but dread those of an uncertain future; while they fear death after death, they are not afraid of death here on earth. Thus, deceptive hope soothes their fear with the comforting idea of a future life.

"And now – for the evil grows apace – the corruption of morals gains ground from day to day, and throughout the entire world those abominable shrines [presumably house churches] of this evil confederacy increase in number. This conspiracy must be radically rooted out and execrated . . ."

Octavius argued from the design evident in nature to the existence of Divine Providence, and he poured scorn on the pagan gods and their rites. He said the abominations attributed to Christians were those of pagans and their gods (the accusations about them may have been made originally by one group of Christians against another – heretical – group), and he claimed that Christian conduct was exemplary: ". . . with a good heart we cling to the bond of one marriage; in our desire for offspring we have only one wife or none at all. The banquets we conduct are distinguished not only by their modesty, but also by their soberness . . . Chaste in conversation and even more chaste in body, very many enjoy the perpetual virginity of a body undefiled rather than boast of it . . .

". . . the fact that our number is increasing daily does not furnish any proof of error, but testifies to a conduct deserving praise . . . we practise mutual love, because we do not know how to hate; and to your displeasure, we call ourselves brethren, as being human children of one divine Father, sharers in one faith, and joint heirs of the same hope."

Caecilius was converted by Octavius's arguments. It could be said that this was a foregone conclusion, but Octavius argued cogently in asserting Christianity's superiority. More remarkable still is his Romanness. He seems closer to Cicero than to Paul of Tarsus; if he, rather than Paul, had to preach on the Acropolis, he would have tried to convince the Greeks of Jesus Christ's supreme reasonableness. He prizes Christianity for its moral impact. Christ, the Cross and the New Testament are downplayed. Christianity has been grafted effortlessly onto classical Rome as a surer moral guide than Stoicism. Given Octavius's audience, it was an effective apologetic approach, but it had disquieting implications. Octavius did not face the objection that Christians worship a criminal who died on a cross. He balked at the scandal of the cross and pointed instead to the pagan worship of wooden idols, which suggests crucifixion was still a problem for him. Paul of Tarsus would not have let such an opportunity pass. Octavius, even though Christian, was imbued with society's aristocratic ethos, which conditioned his understanding of the faith. The cultural conditioning made him shy away from full acceptance of Christ's humanity.

Minucius Felix, who wrote at the end of the second or the beginning of the third century, was the first Christian author in Rome, and perhaps the first of all, to write in Latin rather than Greek. This contradicted Caecilius's criticism of Christians as aliens. Minucius Felix's balanced phrases are perfectly in keeping with Roman notions of decorum. One can see him gathering his toga as he paddled at Ostia. Was he thoroughly assimilated, then, to pagan Rome? No; he radically critized Roman history, which pagans took as proof of the gods' validity. He ridiculed "glorious and celebrated Roman justice" and its history, which "began with a partnership in crime ... [Romans] owed their growth in power to the immunity resulting from the terror of their savagery."

Romans, proud of having extended the city's rule over the known world, were used to reverence for their history. Like other imperial powers, Rome expected gratitude from those it had subjugated. Minucius Felix, however, gave voice, in an impeccable Roman accent, to the view of those subjected. Perhaps the pagans' suspicion of Roman Christians was justified. Minucius Felix's biting words recall those of the Caledonian chief Calgacus in AD 83 as quoted by Tacitus: "... you find in them [the Romans] an arrogance which no reasonable submission can elude. Brigands of the world, they have exhausted the land by their indiscriminate plunder, and now they ransack the sea. The wealth of an enemy excites their cupidity, his poverty their lust of power. East and West have failed to glut their maw. They are unique in being as violently tempted to attack the poor as the wealthy. Robbery, butchery, rapine, the liars call Empire; they create a desolation and call it peace."

Although Christians as a whole respected civil authority, many felt the harshness of Roman rule. During later presecutions, in fact, some Christians fled to the barbarians, evidently considering them less barbarous than the Romans. Minucius Felix shows that while Christians could be thoroughly Roman, they were also insiders who remained outsiders.

Adoption of Latin distinguished Christians in Rome from Greek-speaking Christians, as did a related development: in Rome, Christians began to celebrate Easter, but unlike most

Christians of Asia Minor, they decided it must always be on a Sunday rather than on the same day as the Jewish Passover. The Roman practice coincided with that of Alexandria. The difference in the date of celebration caused controversy, but in AD 190 Bishop Victor of Rome demanded that all other churches adopt the Roman practice, which he apparently believed was inherited from Peter and Paul. His strong stand may have been partly due to concern about immigrants from Asia Minor in Rome, who, led by a priest named Blastus, tried to introduce the Eastern calculation of Easter. Bishop Irenaeus of Lyons was one of those who protested against Victor's decree, recalling that only thirty-five years earlier Polycarp had unsuccessfully tried to convince Romans to celebrate Easter solemnly. But eventually Victor won out.

Although the clash about dates was sharp, the pattern for celebration of Easter was substantially the same in East and West. It was preceded by an obligatory fast of a few days and culminated in a nocturnal vigil for all members of the congregation rather than being strictly a family affair as was the Jewish Passover. By the third century and perhaps earlier, baptisms seem to have taken place during the Easter vigil.

About 190, Theodotus, a leather merchant from Byzantium, arrived in Rome. He was friendly with the renowned Greek physician Galen, who was Commodus's doctor. Theodotus and his followers claimed scriptural authority for teaching that Jesus had been simply an upright man until his baptism, when the spirit of Christ, the Messiah, had descended on him. It was a prelude to future fierce controversies about Christ's nature. Victor excommunicated Theodotus.

The first bishop of Rome from North Africa, Victor (189–198) was not only imperious but had imperial connections. His link with Commodus was through the emperor's concubine Marcia, a Christian who "could do just about anything she liked with him" (that is, with Commodus). She arranged the first deal between an emperor and a pope: Victor supplied her with a list of Christians condemned to the Sardinian mines, and Marcia convinced Commodus to order their release. Among those freed was one who had an extraordinary career, during which he was the creator and curator of catacombs still known by his name: Callistus.

12

CALLISTUS

CALLISTUS had been the slave of a Christian ex-slave who was in the imperial household. Christians were advised to treat their slaves well, but Christians did not oppose slavery as an institution. As Genesis affirmed that God had created all men in His own image, it was deduced that slavery derived from sin. Sin, then, was the enemy, and the institution of slavery was irrelevant. The Christian community was the new creation in which the sinful order was left behind: in liturgical rites, slaves were the equal of their masters.

Manumission of slaves, therefore, was considered charitable rather than a matter of justice. Callistus's master, Carpophorus, must have been both generous and charitable, for after freeing Callistus, he set him up as a money-dealer in the Roman fish market. Knowing his former owner's good reputation, many deposited money with Callistus. Nevertheless, the first Roman Catholic bank failed. Callistus fled to the port, where he boarded a ship standing offshore, but Carpophorus was close on his heels and had himself rowed toward it. Although Callistus, seeing Carpophorus approach, threw himself into the sea, sailors fished him out and handed him over.

Callistus was brought back to Rome to work on a treadmill, but creditors, hoping to recover their money, obtained his release. However, Callistus was trouble-prone: he was arrested for brawling in a synagogue where he may have been trying to collect debts. In 188–89 the

Roman prefect Fuscianus condemned him to hard labour in the Sardinian mines.

Sardinia was Rome's Siberia. Christians sentenced for their beliefs were sometimes sent there. Trials of Christians did not always end in death sentences either by beheading, drowning, burning or other means. Other sentences included banishment, forced labour, or, in the case of women, service in brothels.

In Sardinia, where there were nineteen mines, Callistus would have had his hair half-shorn to facilitate identification. The State considered the miners as replaceable implements rather than as human beings. There was no attempt to protect them against the effect of scarce ventilation, cramped conditions and inadequate drainage.

"Soaked in water which seeped into the galleries," wrote J. G. Davies of these unfortunates, "bleary-eyed through the smoke of fires, cramped at the face with barely room to move, bruised about their naked bodies against the rough walls of the narrow tunnels, chafed by the fetters which gripped their ankles, exhausted with ceaselessly treading the water wheels on the Archimedean screws, straining without respite at the mills to grind the ore, all but suffocated in the dank atmosphere, flogged by overseers at the least sign of relaxation, their limbs unwashed and disfigured with filth, these Christian martyrs yearned for death. . . ."

Usually they found it, without ever seeing the light of day again. Callistus was luckier. Perhaps his preliminary spell on a treadmill in Rome had been good training. Bishop Victor had excluded the brawler and ex-bankrupt from the list of those to be released, but Callistus pleaded successfully with the mine's overseer.

Bishop Victor found Callistus in Rome again, where his creditors and Carpophorus had scores to settle. He gave

Callistus a pension and consigned him to Anzio, a seaport which, the bishop must have hoped, was a safe distance from Rome. But in 198 Victor died, and his successor Zephyrinus recalled Callistus, making him his principal deacon in charge of administration and also custodian of a cemetery on the Appian Way which is now called after him, whereas other catacombs bear the name of either a martyr buried there or the donor of the land.

The catacombs excavated under Callistus's direction are identifiable as Area Prima (First Zone) within the complex. Measuring seventy-five by thirty metres, they are in a grid pattern with seven parallel passageways.

About twenty-five metres underground at their greatest depth, their galleries have up to eight tiers where bodies could be laid. A few of the tombs are still unopened. For twenty years, Callistus supervised this painstaking excavation. The diggers are depicted in some surviving catacomb frescoes. Dressed in togas and working by the light of oil lamps with picks, spades and shovels, they hacked out not only the many-tiered galleries but niches of different sizes and shapes – and then hauled the detritus to the surface. Trying work, but presumably Callistus, after his mining in Sardinia, ensured tolerable conditions.

Previously, rich Christians had allowed fellow believers to be buried in their grounds, but now the Church felt confident enough to own and administer its own cemetery. It was a significant development.

What had happened? After he had killed Marcus Aurelius's sister, who he feared was planning a coup d'état, Commodus had unleashed a reign of terror. Marcia had lent a helping hand again: she poisoned Commodus, proving herself more dangerous than the tigers he enjoyed fighting. He was so powerful that even after the poison he had to be strangled in his bath. Rhinos in the capital, like the Romans, could breathe more freely. Commodus was the last unworthy representative of the "adoptive" emperors.

The Senate, reasserting its traditional prerogatives, elected a senator, Pertinax, as emperor, but two months later the imperial guards killed him and announced that the highest bidder would be emperor. The wife of a millionare banker named Didius Julianus ordered him to make the best bid. He offered each of the approximately ten-thousand-strong Praetorian (imperial) guard two hundred and fifty gold coins, the equivalent of two kilos of gold for every man. The army revolted, and one general, Septimus Severus, violated tradition by entering Rome with armed troops. Didius Julianus was decapitated in his bath (his wive became a widow but also an ex-empress). The prestige of the Senate, which had acquiesced in Didius Julianus's bribery, declined.

Septimus Severus was the first emperor from Roman Africa (the Church was prompter in this respect, as the North African Victor had already been bishop of Rome). Born in Leptis Magna (in what is now Libya), Septimus Severus came from a wealthy family; he had studied philosophy in Athens and law in Rome. A handsome, sharp-bearded, honest cynic, he was a successful commander in almost constant wars, as is attested by his Triumphal Arch, which is still prominent in the Forum. He launched an extensive building and restoration programme in Rome, and also provided the most lavish spectacles since the time of Domitian.

He was in Syria when his first wife died. Septimus Severus had a weakness for astrology which led him to the Syrian city of Emesa, where a conical black stone, the remains of a meteorite, was venerated in a famous temple of the Sun. The emperor married Julia Domna, the daughter of the temple's priest. Medallions show her as sweetfaced, with large eyes and an elaborate hairdo. She was the beginning of a strong female influence in the Severan dynasty. It was devoted to the Sun god, which some scholars see as introducing a form of monotheism.

Again, as under Commodus, Christians were influential at the imperial court. When mobs were hostile to Christian senatorial families, the emperor vouched for their loyalty. In 190 a synod of bishops was able to assemble. As mentioned, the Christian community had its own cemetery. The Church was not officially recognized, but it was partially out in the open, more confident but also more vulnerable.

In 202 an imperial edict forbade conversions to Judaism and Christianity. Probably this was caused by Christians and Jews ignoring the public ceremonies held that year to mark the tenth anniversary of Septimus Severus's reign. The celebrations were most lavish in his native North Africa, and it was there that mob violence broke out against Christians, many of whom were killed.

Even if Septimus Severus did not put pressure on the Church in Rome, it was beset by internal problems. At last it condemned the New Prophecy movement of Montanus, whose insistence on the need for continence for all was a threat not only to the family-based Church of believing households but also to the clergy, because celibacy was not yet obligatory for them and the continent could claim to be a new élite. Apparently Rome had decided at last that the New Prophecy movement took worthy causes (attention to the Spirit, asceticism and rejection of the world) to dangerous extremes, but by this time it was influential in North Africa, where it was to win the allegiance of one of Christianity's most incisive polemicists – Tertullian.

In Rome there was a newer dispute over Christ and the Trinity. For a time there was a salaried, schismatic bishop in Rome, while an acrimonious polemicist named Hippolytus criticized the doctrinal decisions of Bishop Zephyrinus, whom he called weak and ignorant.

In 217 Callistus succeeded Zephyrinus. At the National Gallery in Paris, there is a fourth-century portrait of Callistus on gilded glass. Although there are countless portraits of emperors on coins and medallions, this seems to be the first portrait of a leader of the Roman Church after those of Peter and Paul. Callistus has a firm mouth and a full, trim beard. On his forehead, he seems to have two muttonchops. Nowadays muttonchop-shaped whiskers are sometimes worn as sideburns, but Callistus's whiskers begin at his temples and do not meet. A hairless channel reaches his bald dome. All this contributes to a pensive expression. No one can vouch, of course, for the portrait's authenticity.

Hippolytus's dissatisfaction increased with Callistus's election. His low opinion of Callistus is obvious in an account he gave of Callistus's career, which is the source of the information given earlier. Presumably the facts Hippolytus presented were accurate, but his assessment of Callistus (as a restlessly ambitious knave and manipulator) was polemical.

For one thing, he criticized as "inadequate" Callistus's response to a certain Sabellius who came from Libya. Sabellius gained support in Rome for his view that God, like Gaul, was divided into three parts: the Son and Holy Spirit were modes of operation of the Godhead (rather than being distinct persons). In contrast, Hippolytus asserted that the Word was a distinct person from the Father. Callistus feared that Hippolytus's teaching on the Father and Son could be interpreted as an assertion that there were two Gods. As Christianity had opposed the one true God to polytheism, presumably the bishop of Rome did not want the God for whom the martyrs had died to become, or seem to become, plural.

Callistus may have been unjust in his assessment of Hippolytus's teaching, but Hippolytus was unjust also in his accusation that Callistus accepted Sabellius's errors. In fact, Callistus expelled the Libyan from the Church.

Hippolytus criticized not only Callistus's character and theology but also his laxity. Hippolytus was a rigorist, whereas Callistus, perhaps because he had been a sinner himself, was aware that the Church needed to show mercy to sinners. Hippolytus accused Callistus of allowing unworthy bishops to remain in office; of leaving clerical appointments open to men who had married even three times; and of considering valid marriages between free-born women and slaves, even though they were forbidden by Roman law, probably to protect the women's property. With such in-fighting, the Church in Rome had no need of enemies.

Septimus Severus had won countless battles, but he found the Caledonians doughty warriors, and then finally Britain's cold and wet climate proved too much for him. He died at Eboracum (York) in 211, and is buried under the signalbox at York railway station. His son and successor Caracalla was well disposed towards Christians, perhaps because he was raised, reputedly, by a Christian nurse. It is difficult to find anything else in his favour.

Like Commodus, Caracalla was a degenerate son of a worthy father. Like Commodus, he came young (at twenty-five) to power, and behaved as a violent megalomaniac. Again like Commodus, he did not bear down against Roman Christians, some of whom had positions at court. Paradoxically, the worst emperors were often best for the Church, perhaps because they were not attached to, or trying to revive, Rome's religious traditions. Caracalla's one magnanimous gesture was to grant Roman citizenship to all inhabitants of the empire. Augustus, always reluctant to grant Roman citizenship, must have turned over in his mausoleum.

Caracalla began his reign by stabbing to death, in his mother's arms, his co-emperor and younger brother Geta, and then ordering that his brother's memory be execrated. When the lawyer he asked to justify this fratricide said it was easier to execute than to justify, Caracalla killed him too. He also killed his wife and their child. He built the biggest-ever baths, where opera is now performed each summer. Two years after election, he left Rome – never to return. He sought military glory, but in the East he gained only a reputation for cruelty and rapacity – also against Christians – until some of his troops stabbed him to death. He was thirty-one.

Caracalla was in the Roman tradition of the profligate, sadistic son, but his successor Heliogabalus was the joker in the imperial pack. Caracalla's sister-in-law, Julia Maesa, convinced the Roman Legions that her fourteen-year-old grandson Heliogabalus was the dead emperor's illegitimate son. The Legions brought him to Rome from his native Syria. One spring day in 219 Romans saw him borne into the city dressed in red silk, wearing lipstick, a pearl necklace, ankle bracelets, and a diamond cross. Handsome, with large eyes and carnal lips, he was a priest of the Sun.

Previous emperors had been unpredictable, but some Romans' hearts must have withered to see the perfumed priest who was to fill the office which for Augustus was intended to embody traditional Roman virtues. Heliogabalus built a temple to the Sun on the Palatine: he wanted to make it the official cult of the empire. The Church of St Sebastian now stands on the site. Heliogabalus offered to accept the cult of Jews and Christians if they, in return, adored the Sun god. They declined.

He established a female Senate headed by his mother, which met on a site presently occupied by the Jesuit Gregorian university. According to a probably jaundiced fourth-century source, the distaff senators were much occupied by questions such as who had the right to wear gilded or jewelled shoes.

Heliogabalus's lifestyle was lavish: for instance, there were usually five hundred carriages in attendance when he moved. Mock naval battle were popular in Rome, but he had them staged in a sea of wine. He should never have been left alone with a knife in his hand: he attempted self-circumcision and castration. He may not have succeeded in this second effort since he married three times, undergoing a "sacred betrothal" to a Vestal virgin. This sacrilege was too much for the Romans, and some of Heliogabalus's family also, it seems, thought him a liability. In 212 the Praetorian guard killed him and dragged him through the streets before dumping him in the Tiber. At about the same time, Callistus and two of his priests were killed. The mob responsible may have linked the bishop with the bizarre emperor who was not hostile to Christianity. The two priests were dragged through the streets, while Callistus was reportedly thrown through the window of his house in Trastevere, where the postconciliar Vatican offices stand now in a complex which bears his name. He suffered violence in death as in life, and was not even buried in the cemetery he had organized. He was to be the first martyr since Peter and Paul officially honoured by the Church in Rome.

In contrast to Heliogabalus, his cousin-successor Alexander Severus (222–235) was a sagacious ruler. As he was only fourteen when he came to power, the credit should probably go to his shrewd mother, Julia Mamaea, and advisors such as the jurist Ulpian. There had been influential women in court previously, particularly Augustus's wife Livia, but all those on the distaff side of the Severan rulers were formidable, with conspicuous religious interests which were not unfavourable to Christianity. Some have claimed Julia Mamaea, Alexander Severus's mother, was Christian; certainly she was interested in Christianity. While in Antioch she summoned the theologian Origen for discussion, and the Roman theologian Hippolytus dedicated one of his treatises to her.

Alexander Severus, according to a shaky source, had images of Christ and Abraham with pagan gods in his private oratory. He certainly had the Judeo-Christian maxim "Do unto others as you would have them do to you" inscribed on many public buildings. He commissioned the Christian scholar Julius Africanus to build his library at the Pantheon. Last but not least, he granted a property in Trastevere to Christians for use as a church rather than to those who wanted to establish a drinking house, with the motivation that any place of worship was preferable to a pub.

In Mainz in 235 he offered the Germanic tribes an annual tribute if they would refrain from attacking the empire. The army, whose power he had tried to curtail, must have considered this the last straw. Soldiers killed him, his mother and his entourage.

It was the end of the Severan dynasty, which had meant over forty years of freedom from pressure for the Church in Rome, enabling it to play a more public role. The assassination of its last representative, Alexander Severus, who had shown sympathy for Christianity, probably postponed reconciliation between the Church and the empire.

13

AFTER PERSECUTION

ON 11th November 1959, Pope John XXIII installed at the entrance of the Vatican library a white marble statue of a high-browed male wearing a philosopher's pallium. The bust, which had been discovered in 1551 but kept elsewhere, is thought to be that of Hippolytus. But who was Hippolytus? Or, rather, how many Hippolytuses were there?

It is agreed that the Hippolytus already mentioned, who despised Callistus as an ex-slave, ex-swindler and ex-synagogue scrapper, was active in Rome early in the third century. It is thought that he came from Alexandria but was ordained by Bishop Victor. As a Christian apologist he was almost as prolific as the renowned Origen, before whom he preached a homily in 212. As mentioned, he was angry when Bishop Zephyrinus chose Callistus as his chief collaborator. Hippolytus seems to have been convinced that there was someone worthier: himself. When Callistus succeeded Zephyrinus as Bishop of Rome, Hippolytus was disinclined to recognize him, for he maintained that ordained ministers were not valid if not holy.

Henry Chadwick has written that Hippolytus's mind was a "curious mixture of scholarship and foolishness", but he was acute in spotting the New Prophecy Movement's weakness. He maintained that the basic miracle was conversion: the supernatural is discerned in the normal ministry of word and sacrament, not in irrational ecstasies which lead to pride and censoriousness. Hippolytus compiled an *Apostolic Tradition*, which gathered together the rules and formulae for conferring holy orders and baptism, for celebrating the Eucharist, and for the various functions of ecclesiastical offices. The original has been lost, but it became the basis for countless other church manuals which provide an invaluable insight into early church practice and prayer.

Much of Hippolytus's Mass would be familiar to Catholics today, just as would his use of the Our Father and the Sign of the Cross. For instance, the dialogue at the beginning of the eucharistic prayer:

CELEBRANT: The Lord be with you.
CONGREGATION: And with thy spirit.
CELEBRANT: Lift up your hearts.
CONGREGATION: We have them with the Lord.
CELEBRANT: Let us give thanks unto the Lord.
CONGREGATION: It is meet and just.

Again, the words of the consecration, in a recent translation, are almost identical: "Taking bread and giving thanks to Thee, He said: Take, eat; this is My Body which is broken for you. Likewise also the cup, saying: This is My Blood which is shed for you. Do this in memory of me."

In about 150, Justin had described a eucharistic celebration in terms still recognizable today: in the first part, "the memoirs of the apostles or the writings of the prophets are read aloud"; there was a homily by the man presiding, then prayers in common for special intentions. The second part of the ceremony consisted of the offering of sacrificial gifts of bread and wine by the celebrant, who prayed in honour of the Father, the congregation endorsing his prayer with "Amen". The consecrated eucharistic gifts were then given to those present to be

E

consumed or taken to those absent. The food which had been made into the Eucharist, Justin explained in his first Apologia, ". . . is both the flesh and blood of . . . incarnated Jesus". Here Justin did not explicitly connect sacrifice to the eucharistic celebration, but he did so elsewhere.

Developments after Justin's time are evident in the description of the eucharistic celebration in Hippolytus's Church Order. The most interesting is that the prayer of thanksgiving began with versicle and response between the celebrant and the congregation, as in the current liturgy.

Hippolytus also provides insight into the catechumenate and the baptismal liturgy, which were crucial for the early Church. By the end of the second century, when heretical groups were distorting Christianity, and mystery cults were competing for adherents, entry procedures for the Church had been established.

Candidates had to be presented by a Christian who guaranteed their seriousness. If their work could involve them with pagan worship, as in the case of stage actors, astrologers, idol makers, temple guards or butchers, they might be required to abandon it. Prostitutes had to change occupation. Catechumens received instruction in doctrine as well as spiritual training, and were eventually exorcised. This thorough preparation, which could take three years, lent solemnity to the baptismal ceremony in which the candidate was invited to "renounce Satan and all his works". The ceremony marked not only acceptance of a set of beliefs but entrance into a community.

A neophyte who was baptized in Rome about the year 200 would be anointed with oil to signify the driving out of evil spirits and then asked by the celebrant, "Do you believe in God the Father Almighty? Do you believe in Jesus Christ, the Son of God, who was born by the Holy Spirit of the Virgin Mary, and was crucified under Pontius

Pilate and was dead and buried, and rose again on the third day, alive from the dead, and ascended into heaven, and sat at the right hand of the Father, and will come to judge the living and the dead? Do you believe in the Holy Spirit, the holy Church, and the resurrection of the flesh?"

According to some scholars, the Hippolytus who so usefully recorded early church practice, maintained a highly critical attitude towards church leaders under Callistus's successors, Urban (222–230) and Pontian (230–233), and even became a schismatic bishop, the first anti-pope. Others argue that he was a dissident but not a schismatic.

Intra-church squabbling, which took place under Alexander Severus, became a dangerous luxury under Maximian, a seven-foot-tall general who killed and succeeded him. Born in the province of Thrace, he was the son of a Goth, one of the peoples who were battering at the empire's outer defences.

He was ominous for the Church. Not only did he purge the imperial court of Christians who had enjoyed favour under Alexander Severus, but he also purged church leaders. This was a dangerous innovation. Bishop Pontian was arrested. He abdicated on 28th September 235, the first precisely-recorded date in papal history, presumably to allow election of a successor. A certain Hippolytus was also arrested, but some historians question whether it was the Hippolytus who scarified Callistus. Both were deported to death island, Sardinia, for forced labour in the mines and died there.

Maximian was equally ominous for the Roman Establishment. He represented all that the Senate, with good reason, feared. He held power because he had been proclaimed emperor by his legions, but some Romans must have asked what was the point of fighting the barbarians under an ignorant outlander who was the son of a Goth. Indeed, it is easier to imagine Maximian with a club in his hand than a sceptre. Maximian dismissed most of his predecessor's court, but his suspicions were not directed solely against Christians. He raised the taxes Alexander Severus had lowered. Perhaps most ominous of all, he scorned Rome to such an extent that, in his three years' reign, he did not set foot there.

Under Maximian the prospects looked bleak, but the Church in Rome thrived in the years remaining to mid-century. An oblique pointer to this is that pottery objects were being manufactured bearing the images of Peter and Paul, the presiding spirits of this Church which was attaining a high profile. It suggests there was already a market among pilgrims for souvenirs. A further indication of the flourishing state of the Church was the story that when, in January 236, Rome's priests assembled to elect their bishop, a dove settled above the head of Fabian, a little-considered Roman. The story reflected the conviction that Fabian was God's gift to the Church. A vigorous, able administrator, Fabian had Roman organizational flair: he divided the city into seven ecclesiastical districts, which did not correspond to the fourteen civic zones established by Augustus. A deacon with a subdeacon and six assistants ran each district.

Fabian extended the Callistus catacombs and brought back the bodies of Pontian and Hippolytus for interment in its newly-completed papal crypt. They were given equal honour. The story was that in Sardinia, or on the way there, Pontian and Hippolytus had decided that if they did not hang together they would hang separately. Celebration of their reconciliation was a sign of refound unity for the Roman Christian community. But the question still remains: Is the Vatican library entrance presided over by the first anti-pope or simply by someone who was a "curious mixture of scholarship and foolishness"?

The return of the remains of Pontian and Hippolytus suggests that Fabian had influence at the imperial court: the emperor's express permission was needed before deportees' bodies could be brought home or interred. It was also the first time that the relics of martyrs, previously considered inviolable, were transferred.

Fabian's prestige was high far beyond the Roman See. From Alexandria the theologian Origen wrote to him to defend his orthodoxy, which was questioned during his lifetime and after it. But Origen made a hefty contribution to the consolidation of the Church's standing just before AD 250.

Origen was born in Alexandria, the seventh son of a martyr, Leonides, who had been in the habit of kissing him each night as he lay sleeping. When Leonides was rounded up with others during Septimus Severus's persecution, eighteen-year-old Origen wanted to join him before the authorities, but his mother foiled her son by hiding his clothes. He had written to his father in prison telling him not to be swayed by concern for his family.

The martyr's son became a spiritual guide for a group of committed lay Christians. Although barely twenty when persecution recurred and the local clergy vanished, Origen kept up the morale of his group, several of whose members were martyred.

About 212 he came from Alexandria to Rome ("I wanted to see the ancient church of the Romans", he wrote. He was attracted to it rather than to the capital of the empire which had killed his father), and he met the abrasive Hippolytus. Some three years later, when Caracalla was looting Alexandria, he fled to Palestine. At some bishop's invitation, he preached there on Scripture. Bishop Demetrius of Alexandria objected, apparently because Origen was a layman. Fifteen years later, when Origen was on his way to Athens to debate with a disciple of the Gnostic Valentinus, Palestinian bishops again asked him to preach. To foil Demetrius, they ordained Origen. Demetrius, more enraged than foiled, called a synod which condemned Origen. Origen said he would not like to speak evil of the devil any more than of the bishops who condemned him.

For over forty years Origen devoted himself to biblical exegesis or explanation of Scripture's levels of meaning. He is the third century's greatest biblical scholar, but he is perhaps best known for allegedly castrating himself for Christ. Whether he actually castrated himself or did so only metaphorically (making himself "a eunuch for the sake of the kingdom of heaven") is still disputed, and it is now a little late to settle the question. The important thing is that he did not cut off his writing hand: his exegetical, mystical and apologetic output was such that one suspects he never had an unwritten thought. "Who", St Jerome was to ask, "could ever read all that Origen wrote?"

Origen was in close contact with the circle of Valentinus the Gnostic, who had returned from Rome to Egypt. His cosmogony was as complex as Valentinus's, and he was at least as agile in allegorical thought. It made him a formidable polemicist, and toward the end of the 240s he turned his skill against the philosopher Celsus, who likewise had a Platonist background. Celsus had written in about 177; his text is known only through Origen's response.

Origen was still dressing himself with arguments to be worthy of his father's martyrdom, at the same time stripping the lethal empire of its ideological garb. (Another strand in Origen was that the empire ultimately served God by providing opportunities for the Christian mission. Many Christians who defended conscience against the Roman State were also convinced that its authority was God-given.) He was a theologian of liberation, or freedom as it provided possibilities for creativity and conversion, which for him was a continuing process – he told bishops who sought his guidance to bear in mind always that they could be transformed. (In 1941 a papyrus was discovered near Cairo with a shorthand record of a discussion between Origen and a group of bishops, during which he told them, "Know that you can be transformed.")

Celsus, however, valued stability rather than transformation. For him the gods were a guarantee of the status quo, and to propose another God was subversive. He objected to what he saw as the arbitrariness of the Christian God's incarnation at a certain moment in time which disadvantaged those who had lived before. Christianity, with its leniency towards sinners, its incarnate, crucified God, its implicit incitement to dissent from public authority, was for Celsus a revolutionary movement.

He considered that the enlightened few knew the supreme god through philosophy, whereas Christians made the error of explaining "divine knowledge to slaves, the uncultured, and the ignorant". Celsus was a representative of pagan high culture, determined to preserve it from mere people.

As the founder of Christianity was a carpenter, he argued, it was only to be expected that it had success with slaves, workers and women. Christians do not adore a God, he said, but a corpse. No God and no Son of God, he asserted, had ever descended to the earth, nor ever would. He described Jesus as a hoaxer and as a "robber chief", leading brigands. For Celsus, Christians' veneration of Jesus was comparable to that of Hadrian for young Antinous. He saw all Christians as king frogs or worms "assembled on a dunghill vying to find who was the greatest sinner".

He recognized the Christians' strong social cohesion but attributed it to reaction against hostility rather than to their beliefs. He implied that the empire might as well close up shop if all took the Christians' detached attitude to it. In other words, he accused them of weakening society by withdrawing from it, though his supercilious attitude would hardly have encouraged integration.

He had intuited one vital point: Christianity, although not ostensibly political, was fundamentally opposed to totalitarianism because it taught that man's first allegiance was to a transcendental God, not to the State.

Celsus questioned whether Christianity was in continuity with Judaism, an issue still being debated today, while criticizing both faiths for flouting reason and tradition. Although he claimed Christian values – humility, poverty, turning the other cheek – as well as Judeo-Christian concepts such as Creation, were a misunderstanding of Greek ideas, Christianity forced him to seek philosophical justification for polytheism.

Not only did Celsus know the Old Testament and Christian literature, but he had contact with heretics such as the Montanists. His ridicule of Jesus Christ and his caricature of Christian behaviour were surely offensive to Christians, but they may have persuaded pagans who had little contact with them that Christianity was a low-bred threat to everything valuable in traditional religion, culture and society.

Origen's reply to Celsus was an anachronism which became topical. Celsus was criticizing a Christianity which had little culture or philosophy, but it had acquired these by the time Origen responded to him some seventy years later. At this point, the Christian argument with pagan philosophy, which had begun with Justin, took a literary form. Because of his experience, Origen was the advocate of a Christianity which ran counter to Celsus' respect for tradition, order and stability. He wanted a heroic, anti-conformist Christianity, which would be required again during the reign of Philip the Arab.

The son of a sheik from what is now Hawran, Iraq, Philip (Marcus Julius Philippus), who came to power in 244, was considered by St Jerome as the first Christian emperor. Both Philip and his wife Otacilla Severa corresponded with Origen. The church historian Eusebius claimed Bishop Fabian converted Philip to Christianity, but if so, his Christian sympathies did not affect his public behaviour. His reign can be seen as a high point for the Church because, while he left it in peace, Origen reinforced its intellectual credentials and Fabian was still bishop of Rome. But in 249 Philip made a mistake which was to cost him, and also the Church, dearly. Faced with a revolt by the legions on the Danube and in Syria, Philip sent a forty-eight-year-old general, Decius, to quell them. Decius did so, but then his troops acclaimed him emperor, and in Verona, Philip was murdered along with his twelve-year-old son, who contemporaries said had never smiled.

A wealthy and well-educated native of the Pannonian plain (between present-day Hungary and Yugoslavia), Decius believed that the tottering empire could be saved only by a return to the pagan traditions which had made Rome great.

In 250 he issued an edict obliging all citizens to sacrifice to the gods. Their participation was certified, and anyone uncertified was liable to imprisonment. The edict was not specifically directed against Christians, but it hit them

hard. After more than two centuries of ambiguous tolerance and intermittent local persecution, they were caught
in a systematic, empire-wide purge of non-conformists.

"The Church resists strong in its faith", wrote the
church of Rome to that of Carthage. "It is true that some
have ceded either because they wanted to avoid the
publicity which would be caused by their high social
position or because of human weakness. But although they
are now separate, we have not abandoned them in their
defection, and we are close to them so that they can
rehabilitate themselves. . . ." Capital punishment and
torture were used freely in Alexandria and Carthage,
where it seems the majority succumbed. Everywhere
many Christians compromised, particularly those afraid of
losing their property. A few bishops offered sacrifice to the
gods, and others went into hiding. The bishops of
Jerusalem, Antioch and Rome were all martyred.

In Rome at the beginning of 250, Bishop Fabian was
arrested. He died on 20th January, probably in prison as a
reult of beatings, and was buried in the Callistus
catacombs. Commenting on Fabian's death, Decius is
supposed to have said, "I'd rather receive news of a rival to
the throne than of another bishop of Rome."

Indeed the Roman church seemed to have resolved the
problem of succession, which had become a nightmare for
the empire: since the end of the Severan dynasty in 235,
there had been eight emperors in fifteen years, as competing generals killed one another to seize ultimate power.
In the third century there were to be forty emperors, many
of whom left no trace. In the same period, although two
popes were killed and two more died in exile because of
imperial persecution, there were only fifteen popes (and
one or two anti-popes). The emperor could dispose of the
bishop of Rome, but on average, in the third century,

popes lasted more than twice as long as emperors. There was a comparatively orderly succession among bishops of Rome. They were elected by the priests of the diocese and, in some way which is not clear, the whole Christian community participated in the process. Unlike the emperor, the bishop's life was not likely to be terminated by envious confreres, although his authority could be challenged by anti-popes. In general the bishops, with lifelong appointment, were stable and authoritative; other religions did not have figures of comparable status.

After Fabian's death, no successor was elected for fourteen months, both for fear he could be killed and because the likeliest candidate, a certain Moses, was imprisoned. During the interregnum, a learned priest called Novatian, believed to be the first native Roman theologian, acted as spokesman for the college of presbyters. Novatian frequently appealed to tradition and asserted there would be no innovation.

One of the earliest victims of the persecution in Rome was a layman, Celerinus, who was of noble Christian lineage, for a female forebear and two soldier-uncles had suffered for the faith. For nineteen days Celerinus was chained to stocks in prison with scarce food and drink, but, as Bishop Cyprian was to write, he triumphed over the "prefiguration of Antichrist, the serpent in a helmet" (the emperor).

Celerinus was distraught, not because of his sufferings, which had left him scarred, but because his sister had succumbed to pressure and sacrificed to the gods. Moreover, two fellow Christians had paid to obtain the imperial certificate after a partial gesture of compliance with Decius's edict, perhaps offering incense rather than eating sacrificial meats. Celerinus recounted this in a letter to Lucius, a priest-friend in Carthage, who likewise was imprisoned for the faith. Celerinus explained that as no successor to Fabian had been elected, Rome had not taken a decision about whether to reinstate those who had compromised, but he hoped Lucius would pardon them. Lucius did so.

The heroes of early Christians were those, like Lucius, who proclaimed their faith when arraigned before a State tribunal. They were called confessors (of the faith) or witnesses, which is the equivalent of martyr. Some received a death sentence in various forms, but others had diverse forms of punishment. They were still called martyrs if they survived and were thought, by many Christians, to be full of the Spirit which enabled them to forgive sin and pardon those who had compromised. This occurred in various ways. In Rome some Christians found non-Christians prepared to climb the Capitol to offer sacrifice in the Christians' name and then collect a certificate. Elsewhere some Christians obtained certificates by bribing the verification commission. Some of the certificates, preserved by desert sands, have been found in recent years in Egypt. Origen's complaint that the heroic days were past seemed justified. (Incidentally, at the age of seventy in 254, Origen had died of the consequence of torture suffered during imprisonment; among Origen's sorest trials were the nauseous odours, which also troubled many other imprisoned Christians.)

The persecution failed. For one thing, it was an unwieldy administrative task, and for another, Decius had to rush to the Danube to oppose invading Goths. The Roman army was destroyed, Decius's young son was killed, and the emperor disappeared without trace, the first to fall in a battle against barbarians. Some Christians considered God had taken revenge on Decius.

Not only had many of Christ's athletes proved flabby in

the persecution, but its aftermath was traumatic because of argument over the appropriate attitude towards those who had compromised but sought reconciliation. Rome and Carthage, where, incidentally, Celerinus had gone and been made a lector by Bishop Cyprian, were at logger-heads.

14

TOWARDS AN
ALLIANCE

CYPRIAN, who was born in Carthage of wealthy pagan parents at the beginning of the third century and became a renowned lawyer, described his conversion: "I myself was bound fast, held by so many errors of my past life from which I did not believe I could extricate myself. I was disposed, therefore, to yield to my clinging vices; and despairing of better ways, I indulged my sins as if they were part and parcel of myself . . . [but] afterwards through the Spirit which is breathed from heaven, a second birth made me a new man. . . ."

In the catacombs of Callistus is a portrait of Cyprian painted three centuries after he lived. Two features suggest it might be more than a convention: a bald dome and compelling eyes, which seem all of a piece with the commanding character reflected in his writings and acts.

Four years after his conversion, Cyprian was bishop of Carthage, one of the empire's major cities, which may not have endeared him to its more ambitious clergy. When Decius's persecution began, he left Carthage and from his hideout directed his faithful by letters.

News of his departure from Carthage was brought to Rome by a subdeacon. No successor to Fabian had been elected, but the Roman clergy, through Novatian, wrote to Carthage pointing out that Roman priests had never abandoned their faithful. In other ways also, the letter implicity criticized Cyprian. Cyprian sent it back, saying that "the writing, the words and even the paper" made him suspect it was not authentic.

Because of his strategic withdrawal during the persecution, Cyprian had difficulty in re-establishing his authority in Carthage, where confessors, like Lucius in his response to Celerinus, had pardoned renegades. At first Cyprian said that only God could forgive apostasy, but within a short time he changed his mind: a bishop could do so, he taught, on the advice of a confessor and with assignment of appropriate penance. Penance took various forms which were often public, such as almsgiving: it entailed a request to be accepted back into the community and a ceremony to mark this.

The attitude to the "separated brethren" (lapsed Catholics) divided the church in Rome also. By the spring of 251 it was possible to choose Fabian's successor, but as Moses, whose election had seemed a foregone conclusion, had died in prison, the presbyters' spokesman Novatian seemed the likeliest candidate. Instead, an unambitious priest named Cornelius, who may have been from one of the city's best-known patrician families, was chosen.

Cornelius was the first bishop of Rome who had moved through all the grades of the ordained ministry. He is depicted on the wall by his tomb in the catacombs of Callistus. The portrait, painted at the same time as that of Cyprian alongside it, depicts Cornelius with a tonsure, which was not in fashion in the mid-third century. Narrow-faced, he has regular features, abundant hair and brown eyes. It is probably a conventional image rather than a portrait from life, but there is one feature which suggests otherwise – Cornelius has a moustache.

Miffed at Cornelius's election, Novatian is said to have

plied three south Italian bishops with wine and had himself elected bishop. He sought recognition of himself as bishop of Rome, gaining support from some clergy and laity in the capital, and from bishops and others in Gaul, Spain, Syria and elsewhere. Once he became bishop, Novatian hardened his line against reconciliation-for-the-lapsed.

Which bishop was the real bishop? Cornelius, who favoured readmission of the lapsed, needed Cyprian's support. After a tantalizing delay, it was granted. (Cornelius was to do as much for Cyprian, who was likewise challenged by a rival bishop of Carthage.) In autumn 251, sixty bishops and other clergy attended a synod in Rome which excommunicated Novatian. The moderates had won out again, as in the Callistus-Hippolytus clash. Increasingly the church was recognizing that it was not a society of saints but a school for sinners.

In a letter to Bishop Fabius of Antioch, Cornelius said the church in Rome had forty-six presbyters, seven deacons, seven subdeacons, forty-two acolytes, fifty-two exorcists, readers and doorkeepers, as well as supporting more than fifteen hundred widows and orphans. There had been a Christian community in Rome for two hundred years, but these are the first statistics of its membership. Extrapolation from them gives figures ranging from ten thousand to fifty thousand for the community as a whole. It was the largest voluntary association in Rome, larger than any workers' guild.

A "fast-forward" acceleration in the procession of emperors and popes followed. At the end of November 251, Decius was succeeded by Gallus, who bought off the Goths by offering an annual tribute if they did not attack – which let all Rome's enemies know the empire was still wealthy but also weak. Gallus bore down harshly on Christians: Novatian fled, while Cornelius was arrested and exiled to the nearby port of Civitavecchia where, in midsummer the following year, he died. His successor Lucius was likewise exiled, but then some of Gallus's soldiers remembered to kill the emperor. After three months, they remembered to kill his successor also.

There was a danger of the empire being thrown out in the bloodbath. Valerian, a learned noble and accomplished soldier, seemed to promise a respite from anarchy, but as he was sixty when he became emperor, he associated his son Gallienus with him. For Roman Christians, his reign began auspiciously with the recall of Bishop Lucius from exile, but he died shortly afterwards. His successor Stephen, a Roman, was soon involved in conflict, not with the emperor but with other bishops. From the same stock as Julius Caesar, he was a most imperious character. He clashed twice with Cyprian of Carthage over other bishops, but their next conflict was like an ecclesiastical Third Punic War.

The issue was the white-hot one of whether heretics who returned to the Church should be rebaptized or simply reconciled by the laying on of hands. It raised the question of just who were members of the Church. With most of the churches of North Africa, Syria and Asia Minor, Cyprian claimed that heretics seeking reconciliation had to be rebaptized. In the tradition of Palestine and Alexandria as well as of Rome, Stephen considered that heretics (and schismatics) needed only to be absolved. He wrote to the "rebaptizing" Asia Minor churches, saying that they were no longer in communion with Rome.

Cyprian organized two synods which endorsed his stand, but Stephen refused to receive Cyprian's envoys when they brought news of the decision. Stephen even refused them hospitality. For all he cared, they could sleep under the Tiber bridges. Bishop Dionysius of Alexandria, who shared Stephen's views, advised him to be more conciliatory. Bishop Firmilian wrote from Cappadocia to Cyprian, expressing his indignation at Stephen's "open and evident stupidity".

Stephen denounced Cyrian as Antichrist and then used his Big Bertha: the dissidents had better believe him, he asserted, as he was Peter, holder of the keys of the kingdom. It was the first time a bishop of Rome had invoked "Thou art Peter" to affirm his pre-eminence. Stephen never forgot it, and Cyprian never remembered it. It must have hit him like a thunderbolt from Jupiter, for he considered all bishops equal. The conflict was never resolved, for both bishops died soon afterwards. (Stephen died a natural death in 257, while Cyprian was martyred the following year. As the *Acts of Cyprian* recount, Christians thronged after him when the sentence that he be beheaded was pronounced and he was led to the grounds behind the proconsular residence: "There, after removing his outer cloak, he spread it on the ground so that he could kneel on it. Next he removed his dalmatic – a wide-sleeved, long vestment – and gave it to his deacons; then he stood erect and began waiting for the executioner. When the executioner came, Cyprian told his friends to give the man twenty-five gold pieces . . .") Stephen was to discover that, as an Antichrist, Cyprian was no match for Valerian once he set his mind to it. Halfway through his seven-year reign, Valerian turned against the Church. The contrast with his earlier benevolent attitude was so strong that Christian writers were to turn to the Apocalypse to describe it. "And I have two witnesses, whom I will appoint to prophesy, dressed in sackcloth, all through those twelve hundred and sixty days" was seen to refer to Valerian and Gallienus during their first benevolent phase, while a later passage was held to apply to the three and a half years of persecution: "And I saw a beast rising out of the sea, with ten horns and seven heads . . . and it was allowed to exercise authority for forty-two months."

Valerian's first edict in 257 prohibited clergy from performing Christian ceremonies on pain of exile, and forbade the faithful from holding assemblies or entering cemeteries. It seems to have been an attempt to eliminate what was considered an antisocial group by dispersing its leaders and discouraging its members from meeting together. The edict must have been ineffective, because the following year a more severe degree ordered that Christian clergy who performed their cermonies be put to death; that Christian senators and knights lose their rank and goods if they persisted in their faith; that Christian matrons be exiled and their goods confiscated; that the goods of Christian employees of the imperial household be confiscated and they be sent to work on the imperial estates.

Leading clergy were under threat. In midsummer 257, the "good and peace-loving" Sixtus II, of Greek extraction, succeeded Bishop Stephen. When not dodging the imperial police, he worked to heal the breach opened by Stephen with the churches of North Africa and Asia Minor. On 6th August 258, he was addressing Christians gathered in a private cemetery off the Appian Way when police broke in and beheaded him, together with four of his deacons. Sixtus's episcopal chair was blood-drenched. Later that day, two of the remaining three deacons were executed, while Lawrence, who was the most important, was martyred a few days later. Tradition has it that Lawrence, treasurer of the church, was literally "grilled" to disclose information but said only that the poor were the Church's wealth.

During this persecution, as mentioned earlier, it seems that part of the remains of Peter and Paul were removed from their tombs and transferred to a cemetery on the Appian Way known now as St Sebastian's catacomb. If this was the case, presumably it was to avoid pillage of their well-known burial place.

According to a later historian, Novatian, the anti-pope who had opposed Bishop Cornelius, courageously "confessed" his faith before dying during Valerian's persecution. In Rome in 1932 a tombstone to the blessed martyr Novatian was discovered, but it is not certain that he was the same person.

The proportion of Christians who compromised during Valerian's persecution was much lower than during that of Decius. The weak-spirited had left. And there are indications that many non-Christians were sympathetic towards Christians. This had been true during Decius's persecutions also, but Christians won additional sympathy by their charitable activities when catastrophes occurred under Valerian.

Although there was more public sympathy for Christians, there was also growing intellectual hostility, at least among the disciples of the Greek philosopher Plotinus, who taught in Rome for almost twenty years from 244.

The pagan-Christian philosophical debate was by no means concluded. For example, Galen, the Greek physician who looked after the Emperor Commodus, had trained first as a philosopher and found the Platonic belief in the eternity of the cosmos, where God merely rearranged pre-existing materials, far more reasonable than the Christian belief in creation from nothing.

The debate about Creation continues today, as does discussion of some of the issues raised by Plotinus, who was born in Egypt and studied in Alexandria under one of Origen's teachers before undertaking further studies in Athens. Plotinus, who vainly planned to establish a philosophical oasis, an ideal city south of Rome to be called Platonopoli, re-elaborated Platonic ideas to defend Greek culture and attack superstition.

Like Gnosticism, to which it was in part a reaction, Neo-platonism is notoriously hard to sum up. Including both philosophical and religious elements, it was an attempt to cut through excessive philosophical complexity. Plotinus created a system which showed the interrelation of the diverse elements. Just as the universe itself was simple and one, Plotinus argued, so too was the human soul. Salvation was achieved by attaining this state of simplicity and oneness. Although Neoplatonism was hostile to Christianity, it was to give Christian theology the vocabulary it needed, especially for its Trinitarian doctrine.

Plotinus's ideas and work are known through Porphyry, his biographer, disciple and successor as head of the philosophical school in Rome. Subject to depression and tempted by suicide, Porphyry had "an incurable weakness for oracles". One of his contributions to Neoplatonism was his stress on religious revelation, not simply philosophical enlightenment, as a way of salvation. He turned to a series of these revelations, the Chaldaic Oracles, which became the Bible of Neoplatonism and had to be integrated with Plotinus's thought. He was sceptical, however, about the Christian Scriptures and applied some of Plotinus' strictures against superstition to Christianity. His approach was more rigorous and sophisticated than that of Celsus a century before. Successive Christian writers felt it necessary to respond to him before his books were banned once the empire became Christian. If Peter and Paul had quarrelled, he argued, one of them had to be wrong. He found discrepancies between the various gospels and, like rationalists such as Ernest Renan and his successors, asserted that the historical Jesus differed from the Christ constructed by the Church – in other words, that the Church claimed for Jesus a divinity He had not asserted.

Porphyry, who was born in Palestine but lived in Rome for most of the second half of the third century, was intellectually influential and may even have helped to trigger a later persecution. It is unlikely, however, that his philosophical school prompted Valerian to turn against the Church.

Valerian's order to confiscate Christian property suggests that Christians were sufficiently wealthy to be attractive prey for the hard-up Roman administration. Confirmation that Christians enjoyed high status was a ruling that Christian senators and knights, along with their wives, were to lose their rank and possessions, while Christian imperial officials were threatened with forced labour. Celsus had criticized Christians for abstaining from civic life, but now that they had important posts, they were being ruthlessly excluded.

Valerian's ukase may have been inspired by a series of catastrophes which struck the empire. Famine, earthquakes and floods would have been enough, but in addition, the Franks sacked Gaul and crossed the frontier to destroy Tarragona in Roman Spain; the Goths sacked Athens, Trebizond, Nicomedia, Nicaea, Corinth and Ephesus. The Persians, who had been fighting the Romans for thirty years, breached the empire's western frontier, destroying Antioch and occupying much of Mesopotamia. The plague-ridden Roman army was thrashed.

Valerian, at sixty-seven, still dressed in imperial purple, found the foot of a Persian on horseback planted on his neck. (Another version of his capture is that the Persians betrayed his trust and seized him while he was negotiating.) He was the first and only Roman emperor to be made a prisoner. The mediator between heaven and earth had become a slave of the enemy: that was how Roman law considered prisoners of war. The Persian king's huge son used Valerian as a stool when he mounted his horse. On Valerian's death, his corpse was straw-stuffed and exposed in a temple: "his mortal body", a Roman wrote (was branded) "with immortal outrage". Some Christians were exultant that their persecutor had become a hollow headpiece stuffed with straw.

For almost two years since the slaughter of Sixtus II with all his deacons, the church in Rome had been run by presbyters. Evidently they feared that election of a successor to Sixtus would amount to a death sentence for him. When news of Valerian's death was received, they elected as bishop one of their leading members, Dionysius. In his eight-year reign he acted firmly but diplomatically in doctrinal disputes with other churches. He also strengthened what was already a tradition of generous help to distressed Christians elsewhere. The Roman church sent relief to the churches of Arabia and Syria, letters of encouragement to the afflicted church in Cappadocia as well as funds for ransoming Christians in captivity.

Gallienus, who was forty-two when he replaced his father in 260, was a complex figure: an able administrator, a friend of the Neoplatonic philosopher Plotinus who could be generous even with his enemies, he was also a roisterer and exhibitionist accused of effeminacy. (He appeared as a goddess on imperial coinage and, during the celebrations for the tenth anniversary of his reign, paraded twelve hundred gladiators in gold frocks.) He seemed to delight in flouting the values of conservative aristocrats, as if he had suffered from living too long under his aristocratic father's complete sway; and on succeeding Valernian, Gallienus reversed many of his policies.

Vigorous measures were needed to combat the crisis of

an empire whose population is estimated to have fallen to half the hundred and twenty million of a century before. Gallienus had to quell the revolt of nine military commanders whose troops proclaimed them emperors. He reorganized the army, making competence rather than rank or wealth the criterion for commanders. It opened the way for Illyrian generals (and emperors), which enabled the empire to hold off the Germans, Goths and Persians for over a century.

His administrative reforms truncated the traditional senatorial career. Curbing the anti-Christian Senate may have made it easier for him to stop the persecution of Christians; indeed he issued an edict of toleration, and ordered that confiscated church property be returned. At long last, Christians could practise their faith in tranquillity.

It has been suggested tht Gallienus's wife Cornelia Salonina, who was a Christian or at least sympathetic to Christianity, may have influenced him, but his decision was probably dictated by political considerations. Christians were a considerable minority, and, as mentioned, it seems that pagan animosity against them had abated. Toleration could foster social harmony.

Gallienus's reign came to an end when the army struck again; he was slain by officers while besieging Milan in 258. The empire was still under intense pressure from barbarians after Gallienus's assassination, but his immediate successor, Claudius II, was courageous and just, while Aurelian, who came to power in 270, was an able administrator and an energetic military commander, as indicated by the nickname his troops gave him: Sword-in-Hand. He turned back invaders who had reached Tuscany, reconquered many territories occupied by the barbarians, but sensibly pulled back from Dacia to the Danube.

He decided to enclose Rome in a nineteen-kilometre wall, which still stands, to replace the previous 60 BC one whose remains intersect the central Termini railway station. Rome had long grown beyond the earlier wall and had become, in effect, an open city. Now it feared attack. Other cities of the empire were advised to build walls and organize their own defence. The Pax Romana was a thing of the past; the Dark Ages were beginning.

Before a battle in the East, Aurelian had promised the Sun god that if he was granted victory he would erect a temple to him in Rome. During the victorious battle, troops saw the Sun god aiding them. Aurelian erected the temple (where the pontifical Gregorian university and the gardens of the Colonna palace now stand) and made the Sun god, for a time, the most important deity in the Roman pantheon.

Nevertheless, bishops from Asia Minor appealed to Aurelian to arbitrate in a dispute with a certain Paul, who became bishop of Antioch in 260. In 268 a synod in Antioch declared Paul a heretic for his teaching on the person of Christ. But it was easier to condemn him than to expel him from his church, where his loyal congregation would wave their handkerchiefs enthusiastically and applaud him. The bishops appealed to Aurelian, claiming legal right to the church building. They were onto a sure thing: Aurelian's decision was a foregone conclusion because Paul, as well as being bishop, had held high civil office in the local Palmyrene kingdom, which had unsuccessfully fought the emperor. The episode showed that an alliance between Church and Emperor was possible.

15

THE EARTH
LAID WASTE

THE growth and spread of what was called the Great Church, the visibility of its hierarchy, and the quality of bishops such as Cyprian, meant that in the empire at the beginning of the fourth century Christianity was a considerable social presence. Of course, attitudes to it could vary even in the same person: in AD 303 Diocletian, who previously had been tolerant, launched a fierce persecution which aspired to be the Final Solution to the Christian problem.

The fact that Diocletian was born near what is now Split on the Dalmatian coast may have had its importance, as respect for Roman ways and its religious tradition were strong there. Towards the end of his reign, Diocletian seems to have been convinced that all that had made Rome great was threatened by the Christians.

Respect for Rome did not prevent Diocletian from making radical changes in the empire's structure. In 286, after two years in power, he appointed another Augustus – Maximian, a close friend and able administrator. Diocletian created two capitals: Nicomedia near Byzantium, which was responsible for the East, and Mediolanum (Milan) for the West. In 293 he installed two assistants or Caesars in two more newly created capitals: Galerius, whose capital was at Sirmium (now Mitrovica, Serbia), and Constantius, so fair that he was nicknamed

"Paleface", whose capital was at Trier on the Moselle. The capitals were strategically placed. Nicomedia was a bulwark against the Persians; Milan controlled the north Italian plain; Sirmium was in the path of the Goths who were menacing the Danube basin; while from Trier the Rhine valley could be defended.

Diocletian and Maximian could issue laws that were valid for the whole empire. The laws did not require approval by the Roman Senate, which became a mere municipal council. Twenty years after Diocletian's appointment, he and Maximian were to step down in favour of Galerius and Constantius, who in turn would appoint two assistants. The quadrumvirate was more closely knit by intermarriage. For instance, Constantius repudiated his *de facto* wife Helena, who had already given him a son, Constantine, in order to marry Maximian's daughter Theodora.

Intermarriage and the orderly succession of rulers were designed to forestall rivalry. As generals had been killing one another and the emperors for too long, the quadrumvirate seemed a genial innovation. Now four generals would share power, which would satisfy ambition and make it impossible to eliminate the leadership in one fell blow. But the arrangement functioned for only twenty years.

Diocletian restructured the army, the bureaucracy, the administration, and introduced economic and monetary reforms. He enlarged the army to over half a million under commanders called Duces. He amalgamated the empire's provinces into twelve dioceses, and appointed a deputy or vicar to assist each governor. He created a cumbersome bureaucracy. Of course, heavier taxes were necessary to pay for these benefits. Price controls limited the market economy. Workers and artisans had to follow their fathers' trades, while peasants became serfs tied to the land. Freedom was exchanged for security.

Diocletian assumed the grandiose style of an Eastern potentate who rules over subjects rather than citizens. Hierarchy was emphasized in the court, where even the buildings were called sacred. Most sacred of all, it goes without saying, was the emperor – sacred and impersonal, for he represented divine power. He wore a diadem and gold-embroidered silk robes; his titles were high-sounding and endless. Among them was "Son of Jupiter". The emperor was a sun on whom mortals could barely gaze – they had to prostrate themselves in his august presence. Court ceremonies became interminable, complicated rituals.

In the second to last year of his reign, Diocletian turned against Christianity. Until then, Christians held important positions in the court. There was even a large church opposite the imperial palace. Lactantius, a Christian teacher from North Africa who was at Diocletian's court, insisted that the villain was his assistant Galerius, the giant son of a pagan priestess Romula fanatically hostile to Christians. (The tombs, unfortunately empty, of Galerius and his mother were found towards the end of 1991 between Belgrade and Serbia's Bulgarian border.) But it is likely that various factors influenced Diocletian. One may have been that there were recent cases of soldiers who rebelled and were martyred for their faith.

During a ceremony at Tignis in Mauretania (North Africa) on 21st July 298, a centurion Marcellus threw down his belt before the legion's standards, saying that as a Christian he could not serve under military oath but only for Christ Jesus. Tried some three months later, he confirmed his action and words and was beheaded for breaking the centurions' oath.

Marcellus's protests may have indicated increased friction between Christians and the empire over military service. The Christians' attitude to military service varied. According to Hippolytus's Church Order, any catechumen who joined the army was to be excluded from further instruction. He considered the Roman imperium an expression of Satan's power. But other Christians trenchantly critical of the empire, such as Origen and Tertullian, recognized Rome's authority. Clement of Alexandria was convinced that Christians should fulfil military service.

The reservations many felt were due not only to the possibility of killing enemies but also to participation in ceremonies in honour of the emperors, which Christians saw as pagan worship. It seems some were tacitly exempted from them, but the problem became more acute after Diocletian and Maximian proclaimed themselves, respectively, sons of Jupiter and Hercules and, in 300, Diocletian decreed that soldiers who did not sacrifice to the gods would have to leave the army.

They are a few recorded instances of Christians refusing to obey about that time, and there may have been more. News of conscientious objectors could have irritated an old army man like Diocletian.

Another factor which may have influenced Diocletian was the rapid spread of a new religion whose founder declared himself an "apostle of Christ". He was a Syriac-speaking young man named Mani, whose disciples, from about 240, spread his message beyond Persia to India and eventually to China, where there were adherents into the 1930s. In 276 Mani was skinned alive by the Persian king Vartan, but he had launched a world church "for all languages". With elements of Christianity and Gnosticism, Mani had concocted a heady new religious cocktail which worried Diocletian, for Manichee missionaries were having considerable success within the empire. Queried by an African governor about the appropriate attitude to

Manichaeism, Diocletian recommended the death penalty for its adherents, for it was "the greatest crime" to "abandon what has been decided and fixed by the ancients". (It was probably to the Manichees' disadvantage that they had won adherents in Persia, which was Rome's tenacious enemy.) Diocletian was already turning against Christians, but news of the latest religious craze, which had Christian elements, may have strengthened his resolve to reaffirm the empire's pagan traditions.

In Nicomedia, Diocletian frequented a milieu which included the governor, who was to write a book arguing that the first-century pagan philosopher Apollonius of Tyana, who had claimed to have miraculous powers, was superior to Christ; the already-mentioned Platonic philosopher Porphyry, author of *Against the Christians*; and another philosopher-dining companion who, according to contemporaries, used to argue that decisive action should be taken against Christians. They would have constituted a formidable anti-Christian lobby. At the age of seventy, at the height of his fame, Porphyry must have been a dominating intellectual influence. Diocletian may well have been convinced at table that Christianity was a hoax, subversive of all that had made the empire great.

At a sacrificial rite in 299, diviners complained they could not read the signs because Christians in the imperial party had made the Sign of the Cross, a gesture associated with baptismal renunciation of evil, at least since the second century. In 302 Diocletian, returning from Alexandria to Nicomedia, consulted the Apollo oracle at Didyma. From a vast cavern, a voice was heard complaining that the "just upon the earth" made it impossible to give an answer. This phrase was taken as a reference to Christians, who were held responsible for wrecking yet another religious occasion. Philosophers spent year-long stints as oracles.

Perhaps the one who had divined for Diocletian at Nicomedia had decided to damn Christians while avoiding making chancy predictions. If so, it would have been confirmation that prophecy required the conjunction of a canny person and an uncanny place.

Within a year, persecution began: on 23rd February 303, the church visible from the imperial palace in Nicomedia was destroyed and its sacred books were burnt. A few days later, a fire broke out in the imperial palace. Galerius accused Christians of the household, but later Lactantius claimed Galerius himself had acted as an agent provocateur. Two weeks later, a second fire broke out in the palace. The local bishop and Christians of the court were condemned to death as incendiaries.

An indignant Christian who tore down an anti-Christian edict was executed. Other edicts were issued which were like the tightening of a huge thumbscrew: Christians had to recant or be punished; churches were to be destroyed; sacred books and objects were to be confiscated. "The whole earth was laid waste," wrote Lactantius, "and from East to West, with the exception of Gaul, three most horrible beasts (Diocletian, Maximian and Galerius) vented their fury." (Constantius, who reigned in Gaul, was far more restrained.)

The following year Diocletian came to Rome to celebrate his reign's twentieth anniversary and to be honoured by a triumphal procession for a victory over the Persians. He brought gifts and staged lavish games during his month in Rome but was disappointed in the Romans ("He could not bear their freedom", wrote Lactantius). Probably the feeling was mutual. Romans may have looked sceptically at the self-proclaimed son of Jupiter as he paid honour to the Capitoline Jupiter, and visited the Pantheon or the nearly-completed baths which were to bear his name. Twice the size of Caracalla's mammoth baths, they had a main pool of three thousand square yards and could take three thousand people. They still stand opposite the central Termini (Baths) railway station, preserved because Michelangelo built a dome over the central hall to convert it into the Church of Santa Maria degli Angeli.

Romans had seen all types come and go, but Diocletian was the first who had deliberately left and deigned to return only briefly. He had downgraded Rome. True, it still had vast theatres, temples, palaces, noble families and persistent memories of glory, but they must have seemed a mockery now that power had emigrated to the four new capitals. Diocletian had made the city a shell of its former self: Romans could stomach anything from an emperor except the creation of rival capitals. The empire, after all, was an extension of the city. What was the point of paying tribute to Roman gods and then turning tail for a provincial town? The gods would have their revenge. *Nicomedia caput mundi*, indeed!

In Roman eyes, there must have been something ersatz not only about Nicomedia as capital but also about Diocletian's style. Son of a senator's freed slaves, he posed as absolute monarch. Romans could tolerate those who pretended to be gods but distrusted those who would be kings. Although his high-and-mighty attitude was accepted in the East, it seems a safe bet Romans were underwhelmed.

Traditionally, the emperor's rank was indicated by a purple mantle which originated in Dalmatia. Senators shared the purple because their tunic had a broad purple band and the knights a narrower one. The *nomenclatura* was linked by purple dye rather than by blue blood. But the Dalmatian Diocletian had abolished Dalmatian purple, which had shown that the other magistrates shared the emperor's authority. His gold-embroidered silk robes and the obligatory prostration in his presence were designed to emphasize his superiority over everyone else.

Diocletian, who seems to have been personally unassuming, must have thought all this necessary to hold the empire together, but Romans could have contrasted it to Augustus's homespun style. By comparison, Diocletian was really trying too hard.

If pagan Romans had reservations about Diocletian, for Christians he would have been Antichrist, Satan's servant and the Beast. Persecution was harshest in the East, but it was devastating in Rome also. The thirteen-year-old Agnes is believed to have been killed in Rome at this time (after exposure in a brothel, because Roman law forbade execution of virgins) along with several other martyrs. (Blood shed in Diocletian's persecution still flows. Januarius, bishop of Benevento, went to Pozzuoli, near Naples, to comfort Christians who faced execution. He too was seized and, on 19th September 305, decapitated. His blood was gathered in phials and is kept in the Naples cathedral; all being well, it liquefies twice yearly.) The library of the church in Rome was lost, as well as the archives kept on the site of the present Chancery palace where sits the marriage tribunal (the Sacred Rota) of the Roman Catholic Church. That partly explains why much of the early history of the church in Rome is scrappy. The church's cemeteries were also confiscated.

To mark Diocletian's arrival, there had been an amnesty for common criminals, and Christians also may have benefited. Probably in Rome, as elsewhere, there was a desire by now to dismiss Christians, who were cluttering the jails. Moreover, dismissal could create the impression that the Christians had compromised.

In Rome the previous year, Bishop Marcellinus had handed over the sacred books and, it seems, offered incense to the gods. As this disqualified him from the priesthood, he must have been deposed or have abdicated. This would have left the church of Rome without a head during Diocletian's visit; it must have seemed that the criminal-carpenter of Nazareth had been defeated if even his bishop acknowledged Jupiter's suzerainty.

It was not until the end of 306 that a new bishop, Marcellinus I, was elected. In the intervening period, much water had flowed under the Tiber bridges. On his return journey to Nicomedia, Diocletian had fallen ill. As planned, he abdicated the following year. Reluctantly, Maximian had abdicated with him. Diocletian, who unleashed violence against Christians, had temporarily resolved the problem of succession that had caused so much violence.

Although persecution continued in the east for another six years, in Rome, Maxentius, Maximian's son, permitted freedom of worship. However, Bishop Marcellinus was faced with the usual anguished aftermath of persecution: how should those who compromised be treated? How grave a sin was it to hand over liturgical books? (A bishop in Carthage had tried to kill two birds with one stone by handing over Gnostic texts instead.)

Marcellinus, who seems to have removed his predecessor's name from the list of bishops of Rome, took a hard line. His penitential requirements caused a bloody revolt. After an apostate had denounced Marcellinus for disturbing the peace, Maxentius banished him from the city, and he died shortly afterwards. The controversy over the terms on which lapsed Christians would be accepted back continued under his successor Eusebius, who is thought to have been a physician of Greek origin. Maxentius deported to Sicily both Eusebius, who showed a certain leniency to the lapsed, and his hard-line opponent Heraclius.

Eusabius's successor Melchiades could well have chosen instead the name Felix, for no sooner was he elected, on 2nd July 311, than Maxentius ordered that all church land and property confiscated during Diocletian's persecution be restored. It must have been gratifying for Melchiades's deacons to present Maxentius's restitution order to the city prefect; their God was not to be mocked, nor their property seized.

Roman Christians were able to celebrate Easter on 13th April 312 in their house churches, and visit their dead in the cemeteries without fear or hindrance. It may have seemed to them that they had never had it so good, but in fact civil war loomed. After celebrating Easter, did anyone hear the distant sound, not of barbarians but of an imperial army determined to challenge Maxentius's dominion? Its forces seemed inadequate, but it was led by a brilliant young general, Constantine.

16

THE VICTORY OF
THE CROSS

CONSTANTINE was the blond, bull-necked son of "Paleface" Constantius and his *de facto* wife Helena, who was a native of Bithynia. Christianity had reached there in the first century. By the time Helena was born, Bithynia had a good number of Christians, but Constantine's biographers claim she became Christian after him. It is difficult to discern the truth through the clouds of incense they send up. She is described as the daughter of an innkeeper, but some say she was a serving maid. Piquantly enough, a law introduced after Constantine's accession to power specified that such low-class women were beyond sanctions if they had sex with passing clients; "those women are free from the severity of legal process whose worthless life puts them beneath the observance of the law."

Helena had caught the eye of an up-and-coming officer, Constantius (a venerator of the Sun god), whose rank did not allow him to marry provincial lasses. After Helena had borne him Constantine at Nascius (now Nish in Serbia) about 274, Constantius repudiated her to marry Maximian's daughter. But Helena was not the sort of woman who could be put aside easily.

Constantine inherited his mother's aquiline nose, eagle eyes beneath descending eyebrows, and prominent chin. As a young army officer, he was attached to the Nicomedian court, probably as a virtual prisoner to ensure the loyalty of his father, who was Caesar of the West. Christian writers later claimed that at this time Galerius encouraged Constantine to fight wild animals in the hope that he would be killed. In 296 he visited Egypt with Diocletian. He probably heard the anti-Christian arguments of the philosophers close to the Nicomedian court, and saw the Christians who allegedly used demonic forces to disturb rituals. In 302 he was in the imperial party which consulted the Apollo oracle at Didyma: the description of the event already given is based on his recollection of it. He saw the beginning of the persecution of Christians.

According to Lactantius, although Constantine was the obvious choice when a new Caesar had to be chosen, he was passed over in favour of Galerius's man. Lactantius further claims that Galerius intended to kill the son of his rival Constantius, but Constantine slipped out of the palace and evaded pursuers by using relays of imperial horses to ride across what are now Turkey, Bulgaria, Hungary, Yugoslavia, Italy and France to reach Boulogne just as his father was embarking for Britain. Constantius's soldiers admired his exploit, and when he died at Eboracum (York) in 306, they acclaimed his son emperor (that is, one of the four-man imperial college). Galerius had to acquiesce. Constantine was thirty-two years old.

He barely gave himself time to recover his breath before he began a civil war which destroyed Diocletian's carefully-balanced governmental structure. As well as defeating barbarians, he marched on Rome with about forty thousand troops from Britain and France. Raised in the East, he had never seen Rome, but he came, he saw a cross in the sky, and he conquered. On the city's outskirts he had a vision of the cross. Hearing the words "In this sign you shall conquer", he ordered his troops to paint the cross on their shields. Maxentius, who is said to have heeded the Sibyl, took the Flaminian Way and rashly sallied forth from the new Aurelian Walls, whose height he had doubled. He fought with the Tiber behind him and was routed. In full armour, Maxentius drowned, as did many of his troops, near the Milvian Bridge, which was used for car traffic until a few years ago. Rome had good reserves of food; Maxentius had not needed to go beyond the massive walls. It seemed a fulfilment of the pagan maxim that those whom the gods wish to destroy they first make mad. It was 28th October 312, when the gods stood up for a bastard.

Maxentius had not harried Rome's unruly Christians. It was not a victory of a Christian over a persecutor but one episode, admittedly important, in a civil war which was to continue for years. However, Constantine's belief that the God of Christians had ensured his victory, which reversed the argument that the pagan gods guaranteed Rome's success, was gravid with consequences.

In February the following year, Constantine met with Licinius, the other surviving member of the imperial quartet, in Milan, where Licinius married Constantine's half-sister Costantia. As a result of the Milan "Summit", on 13th June 313, a statement was issued in Nicomedia which has often erroneously been called the "Edict of Milan". It explained that the emperors had decided to "give to the Christians and to all men the right to follow freely what religion each had wished, so that thereby whatever divinity there be in the heavenly seat may be favourable and propitious to us, and to all those who are placed under our authority . . . we have given to the aforesaid Christians complete and unrestricted liberty to follow their religion . . . this has been done by us so that we should not seem to have done dishonour to any religion."

Constantine did not make Christianity the State religion. He was obviously attentive to other religious sensibilities, but he went beyond Gallienus's edict of tolerance with a series of pro-Christian ordinances.

Perhaps Diocletian heard of these developments in the huge (215 by 180 metres) palace-fortress he had built for his retirement in Split, close to his birthplace. As a pensioner, he devoted himself to gardening. Where today there is a coffee bar, Diocletian, who was sixty-two, could sit looking down a line of arches to where ships from Rome berthed. He might have reflected that Constantine, who was destroying his four-emperors system, could in turn make mistakes, as in fact he was to do by dividing the empire among his fratricidal descendants. Diocletian might also have consoled himself with the thought that before Constantine other emperors had had eccentric religious preferences, but the gods who had his allegiance had always won out. In fact Constantine's descendant Julian "the Apostate" (361–363) reverted to paganism but did not carry the empire with him. Diocletian's hopes for the continuity of the old gods would have been as mistaken as his religious policy. It was not surprising that Diocletian made mistakes but that he gave himself time to reflect on them. He turned his back on politics; his co-abdicator Maximian threw himself into the fray again, but when Diocletian's aid was requested, the ex-emperor sagely said that he was too occupied cultivating the sturdy cabbages in his garden. Split cathedral is built above his mausoleum.

Shortly after the Milvian bridge victory, Constantine gave his second wife Fausta's Lateran Palace, where Marcus Aurelius had been born, to Bishop Melchiades as his residence. It enabled the bishop to live in a style to which he was not accustomed and put a greater distance than before between him and his flock.

It was a startling change, which was reinforced when Constantine began building churches which made the

Church visible. On the site of the barracks of the imperial guard, which Constantine had defeated at the Milvian bridge, he erected the bishop's cathedral (St John's) beside the Lateran palace, and nearby, in the Sessorian palace where his mother Helena lived, a basilica now known as Holy Cross in Jerusalem.

Outside the city walls he built – as always, at his own expense – funerary basilicas or cemetery churches designed primarily for ceremonies to commemorate the dead.

Adapting the pagan assembly hall (basilica) for Christian purposes, Constantine built swiftly and on a mammoth scale, given that the city's Christian community probably did not top a hundred thousand. (Not only did he Christianize space, but also time, by making Sunday a holiday from 321.) The scale of Constantine's basilicas might have been inspired by that of Maxentius, which was twice the size of its predecessors, even though from the time of Trajan Rome's population had declined a fifth. Perhaps Rome was compensating for reduced status by grandiloquent constructions. In his six-year reign, Maxentius had doubled the height of the Aurelian Walls, erected a spacious mausoleum on the Appian Way for his son Romulus, and built the already-mentioned basilica named after him which still dominates the Forum and until recently was used as an open-air cinema.

Here Constantine placed a white marble statue of himself, ten times larger than life. Its head stands now on the Capitoline hill, together with an outsize hand with two upraised, admonitory fingers. The statue grasped a cross (in Constantine's words "the sign of suffering that brought salvation"), an unequivocal symbol which was rarely used before Constantine's victory. The statue's inscription read: "By this salutary sign, the true proof of power, I saved and freed your city from the yoke of the tyrant and gave back to the Senate and Roman people, as well as freedom, their ancient dignity and their ancient glory."

This seems to have been the only testimony to Christianity in central Rome. The Forum area, with its functioning temples, was still predominantly pagan. Even the Arch the Senate constructed in 315 to celebrate Constantine's victory, which still stands by the Colosseum, was not recognizably Christian. Diplomatically, its inscription stated that Constantine had won "by the prompting of the deity" without naming him. It is a monument not to the Unknown Warrior but to the Unknown God – unknown because the Senate did not want to know. Nor did it want to recognize the demise of the republic nearly three centuries earlier, for it described Constantine as its restorer.

In 323 there was a Christian Consul, in 325 a Christian Prefect of Rome, in 329 a Christian Praetorian Prefect, but most high officials were still pagan. There would be a pagan majority for another century. Temples outnumbered churches for many years after Constantine's advent. A shrine to Cybele, the Phrygian goddess, stood near St Peter's until the end of the fourth century at least, while pagan temples still functioned in central Rome during the fifth century.

Presumably to placate the pagan majority, Constantine observed the forms. Like preceding emperors, he was Pontifex Maximus, head of the twelve-man college of pagan priests. (This may have been convenient when he built over graves to construct St Peter's: as Pontifex Maximus, he could have absolved himself of the charge of violating pagan tombs to build Christianity's greatest temple.) When lightning struck the Colosseum, Constantine approved pagan priests' performing public rites of divination.

Christians could now devote themselves to good works, but for many of them bickering was more engrossing. They found that exploration of the Gospel's meaning was like peeling an onion: many layers and some tears. Moreover, there were fearful fights over rights to authority. To a large degree, they were the after-effects of persecution. If Constantine hoped that Christians would provide a cohesive core for the empire (most estimates of the proportion of Christians at the time of Constantine's conversion range around fifteen per cent), he must have been somewhat disappointed, for in North Africa Christians were at one another's throats.

In 313 an appeal was made to Constantine from North Africa against Caecilian's consecration as bishop of Carthage, on the grounds that one of those who consecrated him had surrendered sacred books during Diocletian's persecution. Constantine wrote the first-ever imperial letter to a bishop of Rome, asking Melchiades, together with three Gallic bishops, to report to him on the case.

Melchiades added fifteen Italian bishops to the commission, which met in the Lateran palace with Caecilian and his principal accuser, Donatus. However, the commission did not even consider the charge, as Rome had already established the principle that a sacrament's effectiveness was independent of the minister's worthiness. The Donatists, as Donatus's followers were called later when they split from Rome, appealed again to Constantine. Instead of responding that the Rome commission's decision was final, he summoned a Council of the Western Church to meet in Arles on 1st August 314. Bishop Melchiades died six months before it assembled.

His successor Sylvester sent four representatives, but did not attend the Arles Council, which endorsed the previous decision and acknowledged Rome's primacy in the West. The Donatists appealed again, requesting Constantine's personal decision, but he wrote, "They ask judgement from me, who am myself awaiting the Lord's judgement; for I declare, as is the truth, that the judgement of bishops ought to be looked upon as if the Lord Himself were sitting in judgement..."

When violence broke out in North Africa in 317 over the Donatist issue, Constantine sent in troops, exiled Donatist bishops, and closed their churches. Perhaps he felt like killing them, but no, he would rein himself in, for that was Diocletian's speciality. A church squabble had become an intractable political problem. God may have made Constantine His elect, but the Lord had omitted to tell him how to stop Christian backbiting. Once Origen had written that for Christians the only thing worse than persecution was lack of it, because Christians became lax. But here was something worse than both, once power backed one group of Christians against another: Christians killing Christians in the name of Christ rather than being killed for Christ.

There were Donatist martyrs. Moreover, Constantine's policy was ineffective, as four years later the Donatists were allowed to return to the sees from which they had been banished. They were left to the judgement of God.

Constantine had other problems on his mind. Civil war had resumed in 324. Constantine clashed with his co-emperor Licinius, who, despite the agreement they had reached in Milan, adopted an increasingly anti-Christian policy. Constantine allied with Armenia, which had had a Christian ruler before Rome, to defeat Licinius. Constantine promised his half-sister Costantia that he would not kill her husband, Licinius, but later he was strangled to death in captivity.

Now Constantine was the sole ruler of the empire. The triumph he had in Rome was repeated in the East, where persecution of Christians had been harsher and lasted longer.

After living under threat of being burned, impaled, quartered or thrown into the sea, it must have been a liberation for Christians to have a Christian ruler – which explains why a contemporary such as Eusebius suggested that Constantine's biography should have been "written on the pillars of heaven".

Constantine, called The Victor, saw himself as God's instrument: "Surely it cannot be thought arrogance", he wrote, "for one who has been benefited by God to acknowledge this in the loftiest terms . . . Beginning at the remote ocean around Britain and those regions where, according to the law of nature, the sun sinks below the horizon, through the aid of the divine power I banished and utterly rooted out every form of prevailing wickedness . . . in the hope that the human race, enlightened by me, might be recalled to the fit observance of the holy laws of God . . ."

There was tragedy within his immediate family. He had his eldest son, Crispus, killed, and then his second wife, Fausta. Crispus was the son of Constantine's first wife, whom he had repudiated to marry Fausta, who gave him three sons and three daughters. It has been suggested that Fausta, to blight Crispus's possibilities of succession, told Constantine that he had seduced her, and that someone, perhaps Helena, then told him Fausta had seduced Crispus. Constantine killed both: perhaps he argued that one was surely guilty. Helena, who was in her late seventies, then left for the Holy Land, where she built churches in Bethlehem and Jerusalem, and dismantled the temple of Venus constructed over the site of Christ's tomb. Some believe she was making a journey of expiation; she set a precedent for pilgrimages to the Holy Land. Later writers said she found the True Cross, which she brought back to Rome, but contemporaries did not record this. There are reliable reports, though, of Helena praying unostentatiously in Roman churches. Constantine made her empress before her death at about the age of eighty. He left some record of his amazing story, but she did not tell the tale of her rise from the inn where she had met "Paleface" to First Lady of the empire.

Helena, who was buried in Rome after her death around 330, seemed more attached to the city than was her son. It is difficult to know how much time Constantine spent in Rome, but it seems to have been very little, perhaps less than five years in over thirty as emperor. He stayed a lot in Gaul and toyed with the idea of making Arles his capital; a governor would have been appointed for Italy. He planned to shift his capital to the East, where he had grown up. He said his Rome would be Sardis, a city of Asia Minor, and thought also of making Troy his capital, which would have brought history full circle. Finally, after a further vision, he decided on another site with seven hills and on the same latitude as Rome but in a better strategic position, easily defensible and with a splendid harbour. It would be a new Christian Rome in contrast to the older and still vigorously pagan one. Begun in 324, on the site of Byzantium, it was dedicated in 330. New Rome became known as Constantinople, which today is called Istanbul.

An Alexandrian priest who had a following of young women and dockers, for whom he wrote theological sea-shanties, reached the conclusion that "the Son who is tempted, suffers, and dies, however exalted he may be, is not equal to the immutable Father, beyond pain and death." His name was Arius; within fifty years the majority of Christians subscribed to his views.

Arius caused such controversy that Constantine held a Council of the whole Church at the lakeside town of Nicaea near Nicomedia. It may have been the biggest international conference held until that time. About 220 bishops attended, but there were only four or five from the Latin West apart from Bishop Hosius of Cordova, who seems to have been Constantine's main ecclesiastical adviser. Bishop Sylvester of Rome was represented by two presbyters. At the opening, Constantine, who wanted to avoid a repetition of the Donatist strife, urged the bishops to achieve unity and peace. Eventually 218 bishops signed the Creed, which affirmed that the Son is "of one substance with the Father". But the words meant different things to different bishops. After Constantine's death, the controversy was to erupt again when his heirs squabbled, and the winning emperor Constantius sided with the Arians.

In 337 Constantine went to his eternal reward. In his crash course in Christianity, he seemed to have skipped the chapter on humility, but at least he lay in state in the white robe of a neophyte. He had been baptized (by a pro-Arian bishop) just before his death. He was buried in the Church of the Apostles in Constantinople, the implication being that he was the thirteenth.

Debate about Constantine's personal convictions, his conversion and his policies has never ceased. "In Constantine's thought", wrote Norman H. Baynes, who called him "the thirteenth Apostle", "the prosperity of the Roman State is intimately, one may, I think, say necessarily, linked with the cause of unity within the Catholic Church . . . [He] has a place among the seers and prophets." Robin Lane Fox has written, ". . . simple fears for God's anger at heresy made him the most tireless worker for Christian unity since St Paul." Others accuse the great opportunist of a management takeover of the Church, of making it an instrument of government, in short of Caesaropapism.

Conviction that the God of the Christians ensured victory would have been a compelling reason for a general to adopt Christianity. But Constantine's declarations show a growing affection for and understanding of Christianity. Unlike

Marcus Aurelius, he responded to the new and was unafraid of enthusiasm. He was an afficionado of theology lectures, which he took standing up. He confessed that he had "lacked justice" until he found a God who could see into the secrets of the heart – a concept alien to pagans. He professed whole-hearted allegiance to God: "I am absolutely persuaded that I owe my whole life, my every breath, and, in a word, my most secret thoughts, to the supreme God." He had become God's "servant" and felt "a duty to preserve Christian concord to avert God's wrath".

In 313 he wrote to the proconsul in Africa recommending that Christian priests be freed from the burden of civic office to perform their ritual, because it "has resulted in the greatest good fortune to the Roman name and remarkable prosperity in all human affairs". (Within seven years he was legislating against pagans who, pretending to be Christian priests, sought exemption from civic duties; they were trying to scramble aboard the gravy train.) He sent large sums to the Bishop of Carthage for the clergy. Other Constantinian letters show how sensitive he was to the scandal intra-church strife gave to pagans.

Some of the legislation under Constantine shows obvious Christian influence, such as an ordinance forbidding branding of criminals' faces, because "man is made in God's image". An ordinance allowing Christians to free slaves in a bishop's presence merely extended a facility already available in pagan temples, but bishops were also allowed to arbitrate civil cases. It suggests that the Church was attracting men able to administer justice at least as well as State officials. An ordinance allowing people even on their deathbeds to bequeath whatever they liked to the Church was a favour not shared by Jewish or schismatic communities. Constantine compensated Christians for damages under the persecution, while a fixed proportion of provincial revenues was assigned to church charities.

Constantine opposed coercion of pagans, "for it is one thing to enter voluntarily upon the struggle for immortality, another to compel others to do so for fear of punishment." Yet he considered paganism "superstition" and sacrifice to the gods "foolish pollution". Divination in private, but not in public, was banned, probably to prevent propaganda. About the same time as the Christ monogram appeared on Roman coins alongside pagan symbols, marriage laws which penalized celibates, childless couples and widows who did not remarry were abolished – which could indicate Christian influence. Understandably, crucifixions and gladiatorial shows were banned. This meant a decisive change in public life when combined with the gradual disappearance, in the fourth century, of the gymnasiums and public baths which Christians identified with naked exercise, paganism and homosexuality. (It seems that, for the early Christians, Godliness was far more important than cleanliness; the baths had been a convenience for inhabitants of the many dwellings without running water. Moreover, the baths had served as museums, and their grounds included libraries, restaurants, and other amenities. Constantine built baths, near the site where the Presidential Quirinale palace now stands, but they were only for his family.)

There were also fierce laws, such as one that decreed a woman who, demonstrating female "flightiness and inconsequentiality", eloped would be executed with her suitor, while her female servant would have molten lead poured down her throat. Jews were considered murderers of God's own Son and members of a deadly sect. There was considerable continuity with Diocletian. An absolute monarch, Constantine maintained the high court style. He was not immune, however, from criticism for social conditions. The State weighed heavily on its subjects, and perhaps its true heir was Czarist Russia. Russia received its Christianity from Constantinople, and when, in the fifteenth century, Ivan III married a relative of the last Byzantine emperor, there was a conscious attempt to create the "third and last Rome" in Moscow. It meant subservience of the Church to the imperial Caesar or Czar, sacralization of all authority, a despotic administration, a state economy and serfdom.

Personally, Constantine is an enigma. He was The Victor who had a direct line to God but had his wife, son and probably his brother-in-law killed. This multiple murderer addressed bishops as "dear brothers" but banished some. He described himelf as a "bishop" for those outside the Church, but was not baptized until he was on his deathbed, perhaps because he knew that, like other emperors, to maintain power he would have to commit "impieties". He was divinized after his death and is considered a saint in the Eastern Church, as is his mother, Helena. The Western Church seems on safer ground as it recognizes only Helena as a saint.

What was the effect of Constantine in Rome? What would have become of the church there if he had not won the Battle of the Milvian Bridge?

Constantine's clamorous conversion led to institutional and architectural innovations. But the Church was already at work at other levels which are harder to document, and not only because of the destruction of the archives in Diocletian's persecution. Origen had recognized the transforming dynamic of Christianity – its sense of the supernatural and of the sacredness of human life. Now it began to influence not only individuals but a whole society. Evidence is provided from a reliable source, Julian the Apostate, who wrote that Christianity had been furthered by "philanthropy to strangers".

It was not just the Church of Constantine but of Aquila and Prisca, of Peter and Paul, of Clement and Hermas, Justin and Callistus, Minucius Felix and Gaius, Fabian and Celerinus, Agnes and Lawrence. Indeed, before Constantine's advent it had been easier to show that Christianity meant love rather than power. Persecution had failed to crush it: within three decades of Nero's savage onslaught, from Rome Clement was confidently counselling the church in Corinth. The persecutions of Decius and Valerian made inroads into the faithful, but both emperors died before they could achieve their aims. Diocletian made a major attempt to crush the Church, but it is significant that a bishop was installed for the first time in the emperor's hometown, Split, about the time the onslaught began. Christianity had spread so fast initially and so widely later than it was all but impossible to stamp it out, particularly as edicts were applied with varying intensity in various places. Persecutors such as Galerius admitted their failure. Without Constantine, Christianity would have continued to grow in Rome as elsewhere, although more slowly – which may not have been altogether a bad thing. Constantine chose Christianity at the end of a period of persecution which gave him what was, in some ways, an unfortunately strong hand in respect to the Church.

Although the church in Rome acquired a new status with Constantine, and the bishop a superb new residence, he was far from being the emperor's opposite number. Partly this was because the incumbent Sylvester (314–335) does not seem to have been a strong personality, and partly because he was not on the Constantinian bandwagon. When Constantine summoned the Council of Arles he did not make Sylvester its president; when he summoned the Council of Nicaea, Sylvester, saying he was too old, sent two priests to represent him. The emperor and the bishop of

Rome did not form a double-headed ecclesial-imperial eagle even when Constantine was in the city. Not only was the emperor a more important figure, but he had his own ecclesiastical advisors, of whom the principal figure seems to have been Bishop Hosius of Cordova. Rome, for Constantine, was only a stopping place on his way back to the East. To work with him, one had to be part of his mobile court.

Constantine's departure from Rome was a favour to its church, as it was easier to resist an emperor's threats than his blandishments. The distance between Constantinople and Rome was also in Rome's favour, as it remained the one ecclesial authority in the West, whereas in the East there was competition between Alexandria, Antioch and Constantinople, where the emperor's presence made itself felt.

Forceful bishops such as Julius I (337–352), Damascus I (366–384), Innocent I (401–417), and Leo the Great (440–461) managed to take advantage of the new situation and the prestige which still attached to Rome, for you could take the capital out of Rome but not Rome out of the empire it had created. Not only did the church in Rome absorb some imperial administrative practices and terminology, such as "diocese", but also, as the civil power dissolved, it took over functions such as relief work for the poor. However, it directed aid not only to Roman citizens, as had the pagans, but to all the needy. When the empire crumbled, Rome still provided a vestige of order for the invaders through the Church, which, on the whole and with a struggle, managed to avoid Caesaropapism.

There had been toleration before Constantine, but he recognized the Church's social utility and introduced pro-Christian laws. Moreover, his conversion made future resumption of persecution unlikely. After Constantine, Christians had only themselves to fear.

INDEX FOR
NAMES AND PLACES